Cultural Disarmament

Also by Raimon Panikkar
from Westminster John Knox Press

A Dwelling Place for Wisdom

Raimon Panikkar

Cultural Disarmament

The Way to Peace

Translated by
Robert R. Barr

Westminster John Knox Press
Louisville, Kentucky

This book was originally published in Spanish under the title *Paz y Desarme Cultural* (Maliano, Cantabria: Editorial Sal Terrae, 1993).

Book design by Kim Wohlenhaus
Cover design by Vickie Masden Arrowood

First edition

Published by Westminster John Knox Press
Louisville, Kentucky

This book is printed on acid-free paper that meets the American National Standards Institute Z39.48 standard. ∞

PRINTED IN THE UNITED STATES OF AMERICA

95 96 97 98 99 00 01 02 03 04 — 10 9 8 7 6 5 4 3 2 1

Library of Congress Cataloging-in-Publication Data

Panikkar, Raimundo, 1918–
    [Paz y desarme cultural. English]
    Cultural disarmament : the way to peace / Raimon Panikkar ; translated by Robert R. Barr. — 1st ed.
        p.   cm.
    Includes bibliographical references.
    ISBN 0-664-25549-3 (alk. paper)
    1. Peace—Religious aspects.   2. Religions—Relations.   I. Title.
BL65.P4P3613 1995
291.1'7873—dc20   95-18715

Jayaṁ veraṁ pasavati dukkhaṁ seti parājito
upasanto sukham hitvā jayaparājayaṁ

Conquering, we engender hatred;
conquered, we suffer.
With serenity and gladness we live
if victory and defeat are overcome.
Dhammapāda XV, 5 (201)

Peregrinantibus,
qui in decurso vitae ipso
Vitam inveniunt
et sic liberi
paci colunt.

To pilgrims
who, along the very journey to life,
find Life,
and, thus free,
[may] foster peace.

Contents

Preface

"... therefore banished him from the garden of Eden."
Genesis 3:23

This study has been constructed in a three-step process. The first step has been a long one, and goes back many years. It has consisted in my many courses and seminars on peace at the University of California, together with talks and meetings on the same subject. Then came a second step—a short, intense one—in the course of which I presented this work to my audience on the occasion of the conferral on me of the Antonio Machado Foundation Prize. And there was a third step, longer than the second, and no less intense, during which I have broadened and completed the text, and added the notes and bibliography—not in any spirit of ostentation, but either to clarify the text further or to show that we are not alone in our endeavor.

In an attempt to formulate a Latin epigraph for this study, I revisit the Persian poet's distich:

> Rahrawān rā khastagi-ye-rāh nīst
> ishq ham rāh ast-u-ham khud-manzil ast
>
> (Never do they tire who pursue this footway,
> for it is at once the destination and the route.)[1]

R.P.
Tavertet
In Adventu Pacis 1992

Part 1

Preliminaries on Peace

Ouden estin ameinon eirēnēs,
en hē pas polemos katargeitai
epouraniōn kai epigeiōn

There is nothing better than peace,
in which every war,
of the powers of heaven and of the earth,
wastes away . . .

Ignatius of Antioch
Epistula ad Ephesios, XIII, 2

1 The Myth of Peace

To say that peace is a "myth" is to use the word "myth" in both of its apparently most contradictory acceptations simultaneously. Myth represents the most powerful of the forces that guide human footsteps—and at the same time the weakest, indeed the most false, thing in human existence. Myth resembles the saving mirage that drives a person to keep forging ahead and not give in to the searing heat of life's desert or to the objective deception that the oasis was not there—which is what would happen when we came to the place where the oasis was supposed to be, were it not for the fact that the mirage ever encourages us to go on, toward another utopia.

The study that follows treats of this myth from one perspective alone: the religious. The word "religion" still bears the scars of history, both recent and less recent. It piques a kind of allergy that has settled within us, caused by the wounds that a distorted notion of religion has produced in the western soul.

Antonio Machado will be our example and model. Machado is a profoundly religious personality. We need not demonstrate that now. The sensitivity, depth, and form of his poetry are but revelations of the transcendent in the immanent.[1]

> Who has seen the face of the hispanic God?
> My heart awaits
> the iberian one, with the coarse hands,
> to be hewn in spanish oak
> by the hot and sullen God of drab earth.

3

But it would be illegitimate to wish to make Machado into a conventional catholic—a defender of the religious institutions of his time, in Spain or in the West:

> Who insults God on the altars,
> no longer mindful of lowering destiny,
> has also dreamt routes upon the seas,
> and said: God is a route upon the sea.

It is in this Machadian sense that we shall speak here of the religious dimension of peace, although I shall make an effort to delimit with precision the terms I use. Paraphrasing the Latin dedication, I should interpret Machado's lines as follows, and say:

> If life is a destiny,
> God is life's way.

The book, after all, is dedicated to those who find the goal at each step along the way, and accordingly, do not hurtle furiously to the fore. Hope is not of the future, but of the invisible. We shall not, however, be speaking here of linear time.

The thesis of this study will be clear from the very outset. Neither the dualism that sunders religion from politics nor the monism that identifies the two corresponds to reality. Our example will be peace.

> Lord, war is evil and barbaric; war,
> hateful to mothers, makes souls mad;
> while war transpires, who will sow the earth?
> Who will reap the cornspike, June-yellowed?

The summary, concentrated character of these pages obliges me to cite myself in order to clarify the sense of what I mean. There comes a moment in life when one must require consistency of one's own thought. Everything is connected with everything. "Consistency" does not mean "system," let alone "logical system." It means "transparency" and "simplicity"—which is not synonymous with "facility." Authors' true thoughts may be seed for readers, but they should be flower for the one who writes them down. I deny that "difficulty" means "obscurity."

> Honor we the Lord who made Nothingness
> and has carved on faith our reason.

I have no desire to expatiate on the importance of the thesis I am defending. I shall only say that its consequences for our culture are not insignificant. What it requires is not a revolution, but a metamorphosis. Radical *metanoia,* of which I have written so much, does not

4

mean one more ideology; it means transcending (not denying) the very field of the mental, of the *nous*.

While Part 2 of this study is of a markedly philosophical character (although it is based on history), Part 3 is in a different style. Just as the second part represents some of the fruit I have gathered from my courses and seminars at the University of California, the third has its origin in my encounters with contemporary political life, and has been the object of conferences, discussions, and lectures. Especially memorable for me was a conference in an Italian city sponsored by its mayor (of the Italian Communist Party, incidentally).

It seems fitting here to recall a sermon of Saint Augustine, interweaving a translation for our world:

> *Two persons decide to go contemplate the sunrise—videre solem oriturum.* (Is there anything more peaceful and beautiful? We all aspire to light. "I've thought about living till dawn," runs a line of Machado. But these two persons are rich and poor, rightist and leftist, Russian and American, believer and nonbeliever, white and black, man and woman.) *They begin to discuss where the sun will appear, and the best ways to observe it.* (Differences of ideology, of temperament, of culture, of religion, of race, and so on. Any further explanation is superfluous. Is this not perhaps the human condition?) *They begin to quarrel, and in their discussion, they come to blows. Indeed, they beat each other fiercely.* (Quarrels and wars escalate: one sees how they begin, but not how they will end. The strugglers do mutual harm.) *In the heat of the fray, they gouge out each other's eyes. How foolish these persons, who now can no longer enjoy the contemplation of the dawn!* (In wars and disputes there are no winners. All are losers. And what is worse, the noble object of their contention—freedom, welfare, justice—has become impossible for them both. The current situation is sufficiently clear: we are gouging out our own eyes.)

These pages are written in order to help convince us that it is beautiful to see the sunrise, and that dawn gleams for all persons, provided we direct our gaze eastward, though it yet be night.

The subject of peace is too serious to leave in the hands of the politicians; and it is too complex to entrust it to religious persons. The subject of peace is one whose treatment is incumbent on Man as such.* Therefore it is a political as well as a religious problem. It

---

Cultural disarmament applies also to our language. I have argued elsewhere that in our present civilization we are prone to use language as a weapon (Panikkar 1986/13). Therefore my plea for a more peaceful use of inclusive language. Unlike many other Indo-European and other languages there is in English hardly any distinction

is something real, and reality itself is not merely temporal, nor exclusively eternal, nor—least of all—half one and half the other. Neither dualisms nor monisms are convincing. Machado caught a glimpse of nondualism when he said:

> But image is never a liar—
> there is no mirror; all is source
>
> . . . .
>
> all the sea in every drop,
> all the minnows in every egg,
> all new.

Las Morras del Zumaco, La Mancha
Epiphany 1989

---

between gender and sex. We say the sun and the moon while German says she-sun ("die Sonne") and he-moon ("der Mond"), while the Latin languages perceive the sun as masculine and the moon as feminine. Value is feminine in French and masculine in Spanish, while the Italian "la sentinella" or "la guardia" could be said to be the prototype of male masculinity. For me the word "Man" means the androgynous person and not the male element which has hitherto monopolized it. It is not that the masculine stands for the whole Man, but that the whole Man has allowed this untoward domination by the male. The solution is not juxtaposition (he/she) but integration.

I consider it demeaning to the dignity and uniqueness of the human person to call Man a "human being," i.e., to reduce "it" to a number in a set: one (individual) among the "human beings." My I is not a (one) "human being"; my I is not just a member of a set. I think I honor the millennia of my matriarchal pedigree by calling any one of us "Man."

6

2 Receiving Peace

The act in which a peace prize is received is of itself a symbolic gesture. And if, besides, a bronze sculpture by Pablo Serrano, of two clasped hands, is bestowed, then the symbolism is even more obvious.[1]

HERMENEUTICS OF GESTURE

Before all else, peace, like this prize, is received. Peace is not given. We have the current and past experience of the fact that, despite all good intentions, the struggle for peace is counterproductive. The struggle for peace generally creates another war, and at once produces an imbalance that, in the long or short term, will cause a new destabilization, which will probably be more profound than the first.

Peace may be deserved, but it surely is not given, nor won. Peace is received. We need a "feminine" attitude in order to receive it.

Our predominant civilization has relegated the feminine to a position of inferiority. And in saying "feminine" I refer, not exclusively to women in our societies, but to the feminine attitude, of which, evidently, women, generally, know much more than do men. But I should like to emphasize the fact that in every whole human being there is an androgynous dimension which, sociologically at least, has been ignored and even scorned in many climes. I refer to the receptive attitude toward life, things, reality; to the attitude which, by receiving and embracing, transforms. I am thinking of reality's deepest trait—the one revealed to us in one of the most

7

universal acts in the universe: assimilation, which ranges from the absorbing capacity of the orbit of eight electrons to the Eucharist; from the force that leads to organic growth (by receiving from without what is necessary for within) to the instinct that leads to a deep sense of "commensality" with things, persons, and Gods. After all, it is by receiving, con-ceiving, that a new being is created.

Since the time of Descartes, to name a noble "villain," we have so taken our distance from matter in general and our body in particular, that as a result, gesture has lost nearly all of its symbolic force. An example is the sweeping invasion of the handshake as a gesture of greeting, which seems to be displacing the embrace, the kiss, the bow, the *añjali* and the "look" or glance. What is received must be received with body and soul. Mere intention will not do. Hellenic wisdom calls our attention to the fact that form, exteriority, envelope, appearance, is the *morphē* that means, at one and the same time, the essence, the most real element, the furthest recesses, of the thing. Content and container, meaning and its expression, depths and form, are as soul and body—which may be distinct, but which are inseparable lifelong.

To receive a prize with both our hands, with our whole being—body and spirit, without dichotomies of any kind—is also the adequate manner of receiving peace, and in receiving it, re-create it. This is not the place for a disquisition on the cultural schizophrenia emerging from a separation between the bodily and the spiritual. But it may not be inappropriate to recall the fact that hypocrisy—existential, and not only moral—is the capital sin of our civilization: an inadequation between the within and the without, between what is said and what is done, between the material and the spiritual. It is instructive to recall that, in Sanskrit, the word for a "lie" reminds us that a lie does not reside in an inadequation, nor even in subjectivity, but in the very destruction of the cosmic order: *anrtam* (disorder).

PEACE AS A GIFT

The receptivity to which I allude leads us to an acknowledgment that peace is received not as something owed, deserved, won, but as a gift, as a present, as a grace. And here the word "grace," akin to the Sanskrit *gurtas,* opens up the whole spectrum of the gracious, the agreeable, the gratifying, which makes us want to congratulate ourselves, and feel grateful. To receive something as a grace represents maximal reception. Now the thing received is received not as a right or a duty, not as something owed or due, nor even as something known. It is a grace, a surprise. We enter the real world, which is the world not of logical deduction, but of novelty, of the un-deserved and unthought, of the gratuitous. Here is why a too-disdained christian scholasticism has said that creation is a *creatio continua*—a constant, gratuitous arising from nothing, without the forceps of history or the rails of the laws of nature. The world is new at every moment, however it may preserve the traces of the past—like those of the demiurge, for that matter, in this worldview that I cite only by way of an example. Nothing would be sadder than a re-ality that consisted only of conclusions of syllogisms, nothing more sorrowful than a society in which gift would have lost its meaning and were no longer in force. To receive peace as a gift implies this whole attitude. And it is in its reception that peace grows and radi-ates, on the outside as well as the inside of ourselves.

But—and herewith we plunge to greater depths—we must wonder: From whom is peace received? Who is the giver of this gift? And it is here that the gift, the present, of peace shows its true face.

Surely it cannot be a gift from oneself. I cannot give myself peace—not even interior, internal peace. Here as well we collide with one of the most stubbornly rooted dogmas in modern western cul-ture: the august dominion of the will, whether it be the will to power, to conquest, to knowledge, or to go to heaven. The sincere and total reception of the gift of peace puts us on notice: the will, in this area, is not sovereign. I cannot give myself peace. Much as I may wish to have peace, and invoke the power of suggestion in order to have it, peace is not subject to the empiry of my will. And if this is true for the individual, it is all the more true for peoples. The will to peace does not suffice for its having. More wars have been waged to preserve peace than to perpetuate struggle. I can want this or that, but I cannot want or not want. Wanting is a given in me. Any intent of peace that were not to be "feminine," that did not come as a gift, but that imposed itself as a right or a conquest, be it in all thirst for justice, will never be true peace. And we have the proof of it in the fragility of such "peaces" as are the fruit of the will. It is enough that the will of another oppose us in order to have our whole desired, beloved peace come crashing down around our ears.

Peace cannot come to us from ourselves, as the outcome of our will; but neither does it come to us as a present from a powerful per-son, or from others, who bestow it on us condescendingly as an alms. I have said above that peace is received. I have not asserted that peace is given. And I now repeat that peace cannot come to us as given, nor, still less, imposed by others. In that case we should feel uncomfort-able, even under duress—in a state of imbalance, and thereby of a want of peace. We cannot have or enjoy peace if peace is a favor bestowed by a giver, however good a giver. Peace does not flourish in the kingdom of heteronomy.

But there is more. In the times of an ingenuous, acritical belief in an all-powerful God, peace could perhaps have come to us from this Supreme Being, who might even have permitted himself the luxury of predestining some to eternal peace and excluding others from it. A goodly part—the good part—of humanity's current consciousness feels this state of things as an affront, to human dignity as well as to the very nature of the Divine. Peace cannot be the gift of a capricious "almighty" being. No one can feel at peace if peace is a favor from someone else, even if that someone's name be "The Other." The Divine is neither myself (pantheism or monism) nor another (monotheism or dualism). But this is not the moment to speak of the Trinity.

Peace is a fruit of the Holy Spirit, christian tradition says; something that belongs to the very tree of reality, although it is something that can fail to ripen and to blossom. Peace can only be a harmony of the very reality in which we share when we find ourselves in a situation of receptiveness by virtue of not having placed obstacles in the way of the rhythm of reality, of the Spirit, of the ultimate structure of the universe, or what you will.

The great difficulty today consists in approaching this gift in this "fourth world" we have built.

The historical human being has lived until now in three worlds. These worlds are not always peaceful, nor even always good, but they made possible a certain sharing on the part of the human individual who dwelt in them. There have been the world of the Gods, that of human beings, and that of things: the religious, the human, and the earthly. Each of these worlds had its peculiarity, its laws, and its ways of approaching the destiny of the Gods, the capriciousness of human beings, and the hazards of nature. Religion, politics, and technology were the grand arts of life. Modern Man has created a "fourth world": the artificious world, in which the divine is banished from earth, the human tamed and domesticated, and the material subdued. If God exists, he must be subordinated to the second principle of thermodynamics. If human beings mean to subsist, they must bend to the exigencies of technology. And if things would make their appearance, they have to submit to their transformation into artificial entities, from the foods that we ingest to the clothes with which we cover ourselves, and the materials, houses, and other implements with which we protect ourselves. That represents a mutation in human history.

Our interest now is to observe that, in a world like that, peace also looks as if it could only be artificial.

A PREFABRICATED GIFT?

And this is the novelty and difficulty of peace in our days.

The new adventure of earth—upon which, until well into the historical era, human beings had discharged an insignificant role, whereas it now appears that they hold in their hands the fate of their own existence, if not of all life on the planet—invests the problem of peace with cosmic proportions.

The capital problem, nowadays, is no longer that of "East/West" or "North/South," urgent as these problems may be. The capital problem today is that of the mutation at which we are now arriving, and of our responsibility to manage the part that falls to us in this same unfurling of life on the earth.

How may one receive peace in a world in which everything seems to be prefabricated?

The most unsettling response consists in saying that the suggested *metanoia* requires of us that we overcome the inertia of the mind and have the boldness to overcome, to transcend, the very posing of the question. It is a matter no longer of a discussion about means, which is what the technocratic mentality reduces problems to, but of a discussion about the very ends of life and reality.

For this reason, the problem of peace is not only a political, or merely moral, or exclusively religious, question. It is instructive to observe that the *metanoia* to which we allude, within a world influenced by Christian civilization, has been interpreted either as "revolution," with emphasis on the political change that would be necessary, or as "penance," thus stressing the moral, or indeed as "repentance," with a purchase on the religious. If nothing comes to us simply given, but rather everything is built, then we shall not be able to receive peace as a gift.

And here is the great current temptation: to wish to build peace as we manufacture anything else. Hence the fact that a profound reflection on peace interrogates us concerning the very foundations of current culture, a culture based on technoscience. Obviously there is no question of turning the clock back, or of feeling the nostalgia of a lost paradise. It is a matter of being conscious of the anthropological change that is transpiring, in which it falls to us to be actors and spectators. The task is enormous. We do not even have the words to use. And it is here that poets have something to say that no one else can say.

11

The Antonio Machado Foundation has had the unerring intuition that it ought to place these studies on peace under the symbol not of a politician, a scientist, or a saint, but of a poet—a Man who creates with his or her word, because this Man believes that the *animal loquens* that we are possesses in the word its dignity and its responsibility, in the face of the metamorphosis of reality to which we must contribute.

3 Toward a Philosophy of Peace

The expression *philosophia pacis* is not calculated merely to evoke philosophical speculation or critical thought. It also seeks to inspire the peace that is proper to all authentic philosophic activity, that is, it attempts to stir up the philosophy inherent in the actual reality of peace.[1]

The expression *philosophia pacis* can be understood in the sense of an objective genitive, but it can also be understood in the sense of a subjective genitive. I should like to say something about this latter aspect.

To claim to create a philosophy that springs from peace itself is a claim that flies in the face of the modern currents of western philosophical thought. Philosophy is customarily regarded as the hunt for truth with the rifle of reason—although oftentimes it is no more than the hot pursuit of clarity with the pistol of conjecture. In other parts of the world, however, we find a livelier notion of philosophy, nor is this notion unknown in the traditional history of the West. An authority as outstanding as Marcus Tullius Cicero, for example, describes philosophy as the *cultura animi* (the culture of the soul) which we could interpret as the culture of the *animus* and the *anima,* the *psychē* and *pneuma.* When our soul is duly cultivated, and our spirit harmoniously formed, then a *philosophia pacis* arises—a philosophy that is something more than a peaceful philosophy; a philosophy that reflects the harmony of reality, and, at the same time, contributes to it; a philosophy that is simultaneously a cause and an

13

effect of peace—effect of peace because it arises from a calmed, peaceful spirit, cause of peace because it increases or reestablishes the harmony of the universe.

Especially, the philosophy here is an authentic one. It is an intellectual enterprise undertaken for the purpose of understanding, as far as possible, the mystery of reality. It is a view of being, and a conscious participation in the life of being. Without a certain connaturality with what is to be known, there cannot be true cognition. A *philosophia pacis,* then, presupposes that the ultimate structure of reality is harmonious. Now, this supposition is a strict tautology, and nothing more. By virtue of an internal requirement of our own, we have to call the ultimate structure of the universe "harmony." How could we assert that reality is not harmonious, that is, that reality could be alien from what it ought to be? For this we should have to have at our disposition a model extrinsic to reality itself, which would permit us to postulate the supertranscendency of "oughting to be." But such a model does not exist, and we have no other criterion available than reality itself. In the last analysis, only that which *is* enables us to measure, think, judge, *what* it is. What *has to be,* then, is subordinate to that which *is.* But this *is,* understood as synonymous with *being,* also means *becoming* and *"oughting" to be.* Accordingly, a *philosophia pacis* is more than a passive observation. It is also an active participation.

It is Cicero, again, who popularized and developed the notion of *contemplatio.* As I have shown elsewhere, contemplation is not only *theōria.* Nor, of course is *theōria* only "theory" in the modern, current sense of the word. Contemplation is at once theory and praxis, intellectual effort and active engagement. "Uninterrupted meditation, and action, are the best of all remedies," confided the great guru Marpa to his disciple Milarepa, that peerless Tibetan saint of the twelfth century. The true contemplative is a person of action as well as of thought. Contemplation is the integration of theory and praxis. Or better, contemplation is flawless harmony between theory and praxis—although, once a division occurs between them, only a *new innocence* can implement that integration once more. This is the *philosophia pacis* to which I refer.

Let us say it another way. Even the old christian scholastics questioned the possibility of cultivating an authentic philosophy without living in the grace of God. The old hindu scholastics, as well, asserted that, without a detached and peaceful spirit, one could not attain to truth. Truth is liberating. To this, modern western culture responds that one can be at once a great mathematician and a

14

morally depraved person. I would object that not even in this case is that so, understanding mathematics in its deepest and most traditional sense. It is so if we understand mathematics as mere arithmetic, as something that a computer can manage (quicker and better than we, surely). But thinking—or any other human act involving the totality of our humanity, such as aesthetics—cannot be authentic unless our whole being is present in it. And our being cannot be totally present if we remain torn in our existence. To put it another way: unless our being is whole.

Perhaps one of the causes of the precarious modern situation is the struggle to reach a philosophy *of* peace that is not *philosophia pacis* in the sense that I have just given. Then we are led to impose our own concept of "peace." However, nothing of what can arise from a human spirit not in harmony with itself and with the world can be called "philosophy," let alone *philosophia pacis.* "True discovery [is] the one that allows me to leave off doing philosophy when I so desire, the one that secures peace," wrote Wittgenstein dramatically in his *Philosophical Investigations,* thereby endorsing the notion—good child of modernity that he is—that "philosophy" is no more than a question of argument. But this is still a provincial, narrow notion of philosophy in the post-Cartesian world.

All in all, the expression *philosophia pacis* contains a program for and a challenge to the very notion of philosophy (and ulteriorly, the nature of peace). Everything is related. *Pratītyasamutpāda* (radical relativity), *sarvam-sarvātmakan* (all is in relation to all), *panta en pāsin* (that God may be all in all), say the buddhist, shivaitic, and christian traditions, respectively.

NINE *SŪTRAS* ON PEACE

I should like to introduce the following *sūtras* with an observation that will be general in character: the *sūtras* are like the many strands in a single necklace: one intertwines with another, and all depend on one another. Only interlaced do they constitute the precious thing we call "peace."

1. Peace is participation in the harmony of the rhythm of being.

Peace does not mean the absence of force or of polarities. Peace does not violate the rhythm of reality. But nonviolence is not a simple passive attitude of permissiveness. Nonviolence means the nonviolation of personhood, the veneration of the profound dignity of every being, and not the absence of resistance or lack of force or even power. Peace does not entail the homogenization of all things.

15

Peace means participation in the constitutive rhythm of reality, and a harmonious contribution to this same rhythm. We, too, are responsible for the harmony of the universe. In cooperating with the universe, we enhance and transform it. This cooperation, this *synergy*, is active and passive, all at once.

This participation, this sharing, requires a taking part, actively and passively, in the adventure of being. The adventure of being is not a linear progress toward a "point Omega," nor is it a regression toward an original, undifferentiated "point Alpha." Peace is not eschatological, nor does it consist in the state of mind of one who has dis-covered the vanity of everything "transitory." The meaning of our life is not found only at the term of life, as neither is the justification of our acts found exclusively in our final outcome, nor can we shape ourselves by momentary satisfactions. Blessed are those who find the goal along the very road. The end and purpose of the journey is the journeying. The adventure of being is not an evolution toward the future, nor pure involution toward the past. Peace, like being, is neither static nor dynamic. Nor can it even be said that being is in dialectical movement between these two states, and that it adjusts to them with more or less dissimulated schizophrenic convulsions. Being is rhythmic, is rhythm. And rhythm is the nondualistic integration of movement and calm, of a striving for the goal and enjoying it already while as pilgrims along the way. Rhythm is the deepest nature of reality, the very becoming of being, which is be-ing precisely because it comes to be.

I think that from this *philosophia pacis* there arises a profound, constructive criticism of the modern situation—a criticism that we can already notice in its ecological, economic, psychological, and political symptoms.

I am convinced that our technocratic culture, in its cultivation of acceleration, has infringed on the natural rates and rhythms of matter and spirit, thereby shaping an agitated, restless society. Thus, the actualization of peace in our days comes to be an urgent, difficult task. Peace means not the maintenance of the status quo, but, by other means, our emancipation from this status quo and its transformation into a *fluxus quo,* toward an ever-new cosmic harmony. Discourses on peace too frequently finish in sublime dreams of an idyllic paradise, in forgetfulness of the fact that the real strength of paradise is rooted in having been lost, and of the fact that the destiny of Man consists in overcoming—not denying—the limitations of temporality that threaten to drown us.

2. It is difficult to live without outer peace; it is impossible to live without inner peace. Their relationship is nondualistic (advaitic).

It is horrible, and perilous, to live in situations of conflict or war of any type. The world is full of injustices, institutionalized or not, that destroy peace. More than 1,200 victims of war have fallen daily since World War II, 2,000 a day in 1991. There are at present, and there have been for many years, more than twenty major armed conflicts in the world. The refugees in the world number in the millions, just as do orphaned, starving, and street children. We must not minimize this human degradation of our race. But if there is inner peace, then there are still opportunities to survive; without inner peace, there are not. Without the latter, the person disintegrates. Crime, drugs, and so many other individual and social scourges proceed from a lack of inner peace.

But the relationship is nondualistic. Peace is more than the absence of armed conflict. Unless there is inward peace, there can be no outward peace. The absence of inner peace foments cold wars and opens the way for acts of competition that end in defeat, which unleashes all manner of deeds of revenge, declared or not. On the other hand, it is impossible to enjoy true inner peace when our human and ecological environment suffers acts of violence and injustice. Without outer peace, simple inner peace is but a chimera, or an exclusively psychological state of isolation from the rest of reality—an isolation that turns out to be artificial and costly. The bodhisattva renounces *nirvāṇa*, for the purpose of delivering all sensory beings; Christ endures the cross out of love for the world; nor is the saint insensitive to the suffering of the universe. No authentic spirituality defends an escape from the real world, and true sages never box themselves up in their individuality or self-sufficiency.

This nondualistic relationship (there is not the one without the other; we should distinguish, but not separate them) exerts, at the same time, a reciprocal, *sui generis,* causality. Have we not at times seen a mysterious, intriguing serenity in catastrophic or unjust situations? Have we not also witnessed unexplainable depressions in the midst of externally optimal conditions? The entire universe is embarked on the same venture. The philosophy of life, understood as Life's own "wisdom of love," helps us overcome the dichotomy between the outward and the inward, and enables us to enjoy inner peace amidst external sufferings and dedicate ourselves to the alleviation of unjust situations without losing our interior joy. This was

17

the message of Buddha, the example of Christ, the torment of Luther ("simul iustus et peccator"), the enigma of the Vedānta (the *pratiṣṭhā* of *māyā* is *brahman*), and so forth: the revelation of the fact that reality is irreducible to any intellectual principle.

3. Peace is neither conquered for oneself nor imposed on others. Peace is received, as well as discovered, and created. It is a gift (of the Spirit).

Neither masochistic spiritualities nor sadistic pedagogies, in whatever area they may be practiced, can furnish true peace. One cannot fight for peace. One fights for one's own rights, or, in a particular instance, for justice. But not for peace. To fight for peace is a contradiction. The regimes that we ourselves impose are not peace for the one who must endure them, be that one a child, a pauper, a foreigner, a family, or a nation. We lack a more feminine attitude of receptivity, in order that, in the receiving, we may know how to transform what we accept. Christ wished that we should receive his peace, not that we should impose it on others, or that we ourselves should compel ourselves to it. The nature of peace is grace. Peace is a gift.

We dis-cover peace, we unveil it. Peace is a discovery, not a conquest. It is the fruit of a re-velation: we can experience it as a revelation of God's love, of Reality's beauty, of the existence of Providence, of the hidden meaning of the harmony of being, or of the goodness of creation, of hope, of justice, and so on and on. "Femininity," I repeat, refers neither to gender nor to women. It refers to the complementary attitude to what a certain exclusively male mentality has associated with positive values. We accept a gift; but we also do something with it. The gift of peace is not a toy. It is an urge, *nixus, spanda, élan,* an aspiration. Peace is not a finished situation, a purely objective datum. Peace must be constantly nourished, and even created. Peace is not available for reproduction like a photocopy, and there are no full-fledged programs. When we say "gift," we also mean "grace." Therefore peace is also a creation. Peace cannot be attained simply by regressing to a primitive state, once innocence has been shattered. Peace is ever a new creation. It is *Gabe* and *Aufgabe,* gift and responsibility.

4. Victory never leads to peace.

This is a theoretical assertion as well as an empirical observation. We have it demonstrated, throughout millennia of human history, by the some eight thousand peace treaties of which we know or that have been preserved. None of these victories has ever brought a true peace. And we cannot respond that this is due to human

18

nature, since most wars have begun and have been "justified" as reactive measures to earlier peace treaties. The archetypes of the vanquished, if not their immediate children, will manifest themselves sooner or later, demanding what has been denied them. Not even the repression of evil can obtain lasting results. One feels the temptation to recall that apparently so simple and empirically so irrefutable assertion of a young "rabbi" of Nazareth about letting wheat and weeds grow together. . . .

Paraphrasing Simone Weil, I should say that peace is a fugitive that has escaped the victors' camp. We already know that justice is neither "our justice" nor only "justice for just us." But peace is more than simple justice. And peace is far richer than a *pax* that were to be a simple pact, a kind of balance that is usually a balance of terror. Peace is not the reestablishment of a shattered order. It is a new order.

Victory leads to victory, not peace. And we all know the lethal effects of prolonged "victories."

But this *sūtra* has a more theoretical foundation as well. Despite all our distinctions, victory is always victory over people, and people are never absolutely evil. Thus, we cannot say that a victory is only over the forces of evil, or over error, or over aberrations in a theoretical field. Beyond the shadow of a doubt, we only desire to suppress the evil; but we also eliminate the author of the evil. We only seek to punish the crime, but we imprison the criminal. "Become not rivals of evil" (or of their author), says, once more, in an unsettling challenge, that same Son of Mary.

But over and above our wholesome precaution to absolutize nothing, inasmuch as we ourselves are not absolute, a supposition remains, which also serves as foundation to this *sūtra*. And that supposition is: the nature of reality is not dialectical; that is, neither is the nature of reality reducible to logical mechanisms, nor does it proceed from contraries by way of synthesis. Furthermore, peace is not the contrary of war. The suppression of war does not automatically yield peace. The conquered cannot enjoy the peace of the conquerors. Peace is not the outcome of any dialectical process.

5. Military disarmament requires cultural disarmament.

We must disarm our respective cultures at the same time as we proceed to the suppression of weapons, or even earlier. Our cultures are customarily belligerent, and treat others as enemies, barbarians, *goi, mleccha, khafir,* pagans, infidels, and the like. Let us add, further, that more than one culture makes use of reason itself as a weapon: reason is used to deceive and convince.

"Cultural disarmament" is more than just a demagogic expression. It is a requirement for peace, and of course, for any lasting disarmament in the current situation. First, it is not by pure chance that western civilization has developed such an arsenal of weapons, in quality as well as quantity. There is something inherent in this culture that has brought us to this pass: our competitiveness, our tendency to keep thinking up "better solutions," without so much as envisioning the possibility of confronting the causes of the problem in order to eliminate it; our sensitivity to the quantitative and the mechanical; our creativity in the area of objectifiable entities, to the detriment of the arts and crafts, subjectivity, and the like; our neglect of the world of feelings; our superiority complex, sense of universality, and so forth. We have an example of this mentality in the very fact that political and even intellectual conversations on disarmament focus exclusively on arms reduction, without so much as considering these other, more basic questions.

It may be that everything that has manifested itself in modern technocratic culture was already potentially present in the cultural project of the historical human being. We must learn the lessons of history, and, inasmuch as we are nearing the "end of history," we ought to begin to contemplate the possibility of a transhistorical Man—as I have sought to explain elsewhere—long before this phrase had acquired another meaning, popularized by the so-called communications media, which are media of information only in the poorest sense of the word. Our time is ripe for this anthropological mutation. After all, at stake is survival.

But cultural disarmament is as difficult, and fraught with risk, as is military disarmament. Both render us vulnerable. We all know that arms reduction is an economic problem as well as a political one. But economy, basically, is a cultural problem. The step from farming as a means of life to agroindustry as a means of financial gain may serve as a compendium of what we mean.

Cultural disarmament does not mean a return to primitivism. It entails a criticism of culture, not only in the light of all the shortcomings of western culture, but also in the perspective of an authentic intercultural framing of the question.

6. In isolation, no culture, religion, or tradition can resolve the problems of the world.

No religion is self-sufficient today, nor able to offer universal answers (be it only because the questions are no longer the same). A cross-cultural approach to the world's problems is imperative. We are still suffering the aftermath of colonialism, whose essence is a belief in the monomorphism of culture. We all need one another, and we are all interdependent in all areas.

It is very significant that, at a moment when most of the traditional religions are ready to divest themselves of the mantle of colonialism, imperialism, and universalism, the "scientific view" of the world seems to wish to accede to the status of cultural heir of such attitudes. Modern astronomy, physics, mathematics, and so on, seem to take it for granted, if often only implicitly, that they and the other sciences are supracultural, universal realizations, definitive conquests of the human mind: "Finally we know that Andromeda is precisely this far away, that atoms are no longer *atomoi,* that gravitation operates in such and such a way, that quarks, biomolecules, chromosomes, and the rest, right back to the Big Bang, represent reality—which, of course, remains open to further clarifications and corrections, and the introduction of new parameters." But we have already sufficiently criticized the technocratic, and need not pursue the theme. Let us simply recall that we speak of peace on earth and in heaven, and not of the value a particular "law of physics" might have in a very limited context.

It will be appropriate to mention here, where cultures, religions, and traditions are concerned, the word "pluralism," representing a topic I have addressed at length in other writings.

7. Peace pertains essentially to the order of mythos, *not to that of* logos.

There is no single concept of peace. We need only consider the overtones and connotations of the various words (*pax, eirēnē, salām, Friede, shanti,* and the like). Peace is polysemic: it has various meanings. It is also pluralistic: it has many doctrinally incompatible interpretations. My notion of peace can be nonpeaceful for others. Peace is not an ideology. "Peace" is not synonymous with "pacificism." A myth is something in which we believe in such a way as to take it for granted. A myth is not incomprehensible or irrational. It is that which makes understanding to be understandable, reason to be reasonable, that is, convincing. It is that on which intelligibility is founded in any given situation. Peace is not simply a concept. Peace is the eminent myth of our days.

Plainly, "God" was once a universal myth. Wars were waged in the name of God, and each of the opposing parties sought to have God on its side: "Gott mit uns." Peace, too, was signed in the name of God. Now peace seems to be the unifying myth of our times. And wars are waged in its name, too!

But a myth is not open to further fundamentation. A myth is

21

beyond all definition, since a myth is precisely the horizon of definition. We cannot separate *mythos* and *logos,* but neither may we identify
them. This explains why the imposition of our *concept* of peace cannot bring peace.

8. Religion is a way to peace.

A traditional concept of religion consisted in regarding it as the
way to salvation, for which people were struggling. Actually, most of
the wars that have been waged in the world have been wars of religion. Today we are witnessing a transformation of the very notion
of "religion," a fact that we might express by saying that religions are
the various routes by which one seeks to approach and attain that
peace that is being transformed, probably, into one of the few symbols that are truly universal. "Summa nostrae religionis pax est et
unanimitas" (The culmination of our religion is peace and concord),
wrote Erasmus in a letter of 1522.

If we set this *sūtra* over against the preceding one, we shall not
be in danger of falling into the superficial eclecticism that destroys
all religious diversity and reduces religions to an all but meaningless
common denominator. All religions are not the same, first of all because they themselves *say* that they are not. They utter and assert different things, and speak different languages. Furthermore, the presumably identical "ultimate content" in question is not, for most
traditions, disconnected from the manner in which these traditions
are expressed. For most religions, the word is sacred.

However, almost all religions would accept the proposition
that their concern is to bring peace to the human being and indeed
the entire cosmos. Every religion understands peace as a symbol polysemic and pluralistic enough as to allow the use of it.

But this is quite a step. It points up the importance of religious
encounters (in all senses of the word "encounter")—not in their
doctrinal aspects, for our purposes, but in terms of a more existential attitude, and this makes for a fruitful cooperation among religions in our present human situation. In the past, religions were a
factor of inner peace for their followers and outer war for others. This
inconsistency is so patent today that even the religions' own self-
interpretation is beginning to be modified in the direction indicated.

Here it will be in order to cite, in a context of this relationship
between peace and religion, a difficult word: the word "revolution."
The path to peace is not an easy one. It is a revolutionary, disconcert-
ing, challenging path, a path requiring the suppression of injustice,
selfishness, greed. History demonstrates that, when religions are no

22

longer revolutionary, first they degenerate and cease to carry out their commission, then the revolution itself is degraded to a simple changing of the guard. The difficulty of the problems nowadays is immense.

9. Only forgiveness, reconciliation, and ongoing dialogue lead to peace and shatter the law of karma.

This is a historical observation, and an anthropological and theologico-philosophical truth. Punishment, restitution, and reparation do not lead to peace. To believe that a simple reestablishment of the order that has been violated will right the situation is a crudely mechanistic, immature way of thinking. Lost innocence calls for a new innocence, and not a retreat to a paradise of dreams. No manner of compensation can undo what is already done. Peace is not restoration. Human history is dynamic. The very cosmos, while it moves rhythmically, does so without repeating itself. The *status ante* is an impossibility.

The only way to peace is a way "ahead," and not a way "back." But in order to move ahead we must sometimes burn our bridges behind us. This is forgiveness. Its difficulty resides in its transcendence of the first dogma of modernity: the will. Having the will to forgive is not the same as forgiving. In order to be able to forgive, one must have a strength that is beyond the mechanical order of action and reaction: one needs the Holy Spirit. *Karunā, charis,* love, and so on, do not consist simply in the good sentiments of a few individuals. They are the pillars of the universe.

It is instructive to notice that each time the raised Christ appears to his disciples he gives them peace; and that whenever he gives them the power to forgive he gives them the power of the Holy Spirit. At times, only by shaming the holders of justice is the law of *karma* overcome: "Woman, where have your accusers gone?"

The consequences of all of this are so incalculable that it would be improper to try to list them here.

THE CHALLENGE OF *PHILOSOPHIA PACIS*

It is easy enough to refer to Ashoka's edict of peace (the victory of *dhamma,* as he calls it), or to condemn Flavius Vegetius Renatus's "Qui desiderat pacem, praeparet bellum" (Let the one who desires peace prepare for war), or to cite Pindar's celebrated aphorism, "Dulce bellum inexpertis" (War is sweet only to those who have not tried it), or even repeat Erasmus's statement in the exordium of his *Querela Pacis* (that peace is the "font of all felicity"), and to recall the many noble souls who have discovered the central importance of peace in all eras and climes. The true challenge arises when it befalls us to have to act in accordance with this discovery, without any support other than that of our conscience.

The spoken word is always more powerful than the written phrase. I should like to communicate something more than simple ideas. I should like to make it understood that we are all authors of the word, and not hearers only. Acts, too, are more powerful than simple words. I should like to communicate the sensation that all of us, writers and readers alike, are committed to one of the most fascinating, most difficult, and most promising tasks of life, and one that is for everyone to perform: the creation of peace.

As we have yet to see, the problem of peace is not solved merely by having an efficient administration, since it affects the ultimate foundations of human culture, and in the last analysis, those of reality itself. It is a question that concerns us all.

Even western classical antiquity left it in writing. Very convincingly, Italo Lana (1991) denies, supporting his position with an abundant bibliography, that, for classical authors, peace was only the absence of war. This is scarcely less evident for many traditional civilizations. Aristotle himself declares peace to be the very end of the *polis* (*Politics,* book 7). Indeed, peace is bound up with the cosmic order, and human peace is our share in that order. Then we are in our place, we realize our end. To live in peace is the end of life itself.

Peace is not a means, but an end. Peace is not the simple absence of war (of whatever kind) and the opportunity to devote ourselves to our ordinary affairs and chores. Peace is not "there" to be used: it is not an *ad usum* value, Saint Bonaventure would say, but an *ad fructum* one: it has been given us—it is a gift, then—in order that we may enjoy and delight in it. It is not an *uti*, but a *frui:* It is not a means, but an end. I do not have peace in order thereupon to go do something else; rather, I *am* peace (to paraphrase Ephesians 2:14), and, being peace, I live the fullness of life.

But here is the difficulty of actualizing that peace in a civilization that has all but atrophied in us any sense of true joy, of "fruition"—of *delectatio,* as the Renaissance would have it.

If peace is regarded only as a means, then it is scarcely to be wondered at that we, in our so-called times of peace, should go in quest of something more interesting, and end up at war again. Here is manifested the political strength of contemplation: it discovers to us that what so many today call "quality of life" means something more than hedonistic refinement. Life has its meaning in being lived, and not merely in spending one's life in creating conditions of life for the future or for others.

I have said, "contemplation," because none of this is possible without a transcending of linear time—without an experience of life bare, so to speak, of being itself, of naked life. And this goes hand in hand with life's most elementary functions, which, as a matter of fact, are also the most fundamental.

The awareness that life is an end in itself has been too much lost. It is a truth as simple as it is difficult. The great religious alienation consists in believing that true life is the future life, and in seeking immortality in the future. This is not eternal life, the fullness of life. But a deeper degradation still is the scientific caricature that presents life to us as a simple project for the future, that never stops moving, in which everything is a means to a utopian, unattainable end, with ourselves as mere links in an evolutionary chain.

The arms race is a sign. But so is the knowledge race. The very word "race" should have put us on our guard. Life is not for racing, but for living.

The idea of peace, too, can degenerate, obviously. Two great examples, perhaps—which I relate with irony and a sense of history—are the *pax romana,* and the "new international order" of the so-called *pax americana.* The former was based on a belief in the protection of the "civilized" world—that of the *civis,* Rome—from the barbarians. The latter attempts to justify itself with similar arguments, appealing to the *defense* of democracy and "free trade."

The notion, the fact, that peace is an end also means that we must not resign ourselves to positing it at the term of life, in death, in the beyond. That there is or can be a perfect eschatological peace does not imply that we ought to await the *eschaton* in order to enjoy a peace that may be genuine, if imperfect. In christian terms: the resurrection, which is not a resurrection of souls but of bodies, is not only an eschatological dogma, but a hope of the present that enables us to have full joy here and now (John 16:24). Its homeomorphic equivalent is the shivaitic *jīvan-mukta.*

I have dedicated this book to those who have already found the goal along the way: to those who have arrived, and who no longer run. Their journey is a stroll, and so they are ready to go anywhere. They are the "peacemakers" of the Beatitudes. They no longer feel anxious to accomplish great exploits, and have time for everything. The eschatological ardor of the first christians is understandable. But now that the *parousia* has not arrived, we ought to have grasped the gospel message more in depth. Not that we are to sit with our arms folded. Quite the contrary: not having our hands busy with ourselves and our selfish concerns, we are free to devote ourselves to that which we believe to be most important: peace.

25

Part 2

The Religious Dimension of Political Peace

*Yad eveha tad amutra,
yad amutra tad anviha*

Here just as there,
there just as here

Katha Upanishad II, 1, 10

*Hōs en ouranō
kai epi gēs*

So in heaven
as on earth[1]

Matthew 6:10

When human beings sunder their relationship with earth, seeking to be sufficient unto themselves, they turn into monsters. Wishing to dominate the earth, they destroy themselves. Contemporary ecological awareness tells us something of this.[2] When human beings sunder their relationship with the heavens, seeking to guide and govern themselves, they are transformed into automata that destroy others. The concrete historical situation of our day shows us this palpably. The cosmotheandric correlation is constitutive of reality.[3]

The two citations that serve as an epigraph in Part 2, to which we could have added parallel assertions from nearly all cultures, tell us that Man's activity, indeed our very nature, is constitutively related to the whole universe, as we are also reminded by the epigraph of Part 1. All of this inclines us to think that peace is more than just a political matter, and leads us to suspect that perhaps the precariousness of political peace has deeper roots than those of the defective transmission of our political machinery.

4 Religious Peace and Intercultural Dialogue

WAR AS A RELIGIOUS PROBLEM

From time immemorial, war has constituted a religious problem. By contrast, social peace, until recently, has been regarded as primarily a political matter.

Most wars have worn an expressly religious face, or at least have been assigned a religious justification.[1]

Religious wars, on the one hand, and the numerous attempted justifications of war, on the other, testify to the truth of this assertion. The European wars of the close of the Middle Ages, and Iran's recent islamic revolution, are examples of religious wars. World War II and the American war in Vietnam can serve as examples of wars that are not explicitly religious but that nevertheless have a religious character. These latter were not wars of conquest, nor were they waged only for economic purposes. They had a religious *ethos:* the rescue of Civilization, Freedom, Democracy, all with capital letters. The last Spanish civil war, on one side, bore the name of "crusade," and on the other side, at least in the beginning, had a markedly anti-religious character—concretely, against the institutional catholic church. The recent Persian Gulf War, which may have been rather a war of economics and political domination, saw itself to a large extent justified, by both sides, in terms of religious motives, and with a theistic language in both cases.

We adduce these recent, western historical examples because, in other traditions, in which there is no explicit separation of the religious and the political, any war is civil (secular) and religious at the same time.

Those who undertake religious wars nearly always appeal to the name of God or say that they are carrying out God's will, attempt to justify themselves in terms of the defense of a particular religious confession, and in general try to show that the war in question is being waged for a religious cause.

In the case of nonreligious wars, an immediate political reason is given, but in the background, generally speaking, lurks a transcendent, that is, religious, motive. Hitler wanted to be rid of the judeo-christian God of the West, and thereby to put a new stamp on the world. The Allies wished to defend their sacrosanct rights to liberty, independence, and identity. Even a Jean-Paul Sartre wrote on religious subjects when he was in the French resistance. The United States regards itself as the successor to the chosen people of the Old Testament, defending democracy and freedom in the name of God, saving the world from false Gods.[2]

From time immemorial, almost all religious institutions have blessed military undertakings. And the directors of the wars, too, have desired to receive the blessings of these respective religious institutions. Yahweh is the Lord of Hosts, though these be heavenly armies. To limit ourselves to the West, the Pope crowned not only Charlemagne and Charles V but Napoleon as well. The catholic church supported Franco's civil war. Peace treaties were usually signed in the name of God. For centuries, the usual formula in the West was: "In nomine sanctae et indivisae Trinitatis" (In the Name of the Holy and Undivided Trinity). The Peace Treaty of Westphalia, in 1648, sought to guarantee, in its first article, "pax christiana universalis perpetua" (perpetual, universal christian peace). And so on.

A treaty of peace meant the end of a war. But it was actually still part of the war, not of the peace.

In a word, war is a religious problem, although, on the other hand, religious awareness can declare itself against war.[3] And indeed, the first conscientious objections to modern military service were religious objections. The theological disputes that arose in sixteenth-century Spain over whether to justify or condemn the conquest of America constitute a noteworthy example of the theological problem of war.[4]

There are also ethnic wars, naturally. But even these, very frequently, are of a religious nature: the tribe itself attempted to justify its warlike acts by means of an appeal to religious motives.[5]

The religious character of war is manifest. War is a limit situation. The human being and human society see themselves faced with the ultimate problems of death, life, justice, fidelity, obedience, and so forth. In a word: from the first, war has been a religious phenomenon. The Gods made war. And nearly always they wore the emblems and bore the standards of their respective religions. The oracle had to be consulted, and priests imparted their blessings. The cross and the sword were joined for centuries.[6] "Dieu le veut" (God wills it!), "Gott mit uns" (God is with us!), "In God we trust," "Sancta Maria," have been war cries, and have been used in attempted justifications of war.[7] This union between religion and politics has prevailed in Asia and Africa as well, although it is a more accentuated phenomenon in the Abrahamic religions precisely because of the sharper distinction between the sacred and the profane. The autonomy of the "secular arm" requires the support of sacred authority in matters of life and death.

To put it another way: political war, too, at bottom, was religious war. Be the motives for a war economic, nationalistic, or other, religion was always to be found at the center. No prince would have dared start a war without first consulting the oracles, prophets, astrologers, or priests. In some cases, and in many senses, war was like a ritual act.[8]

Seen from the viewpoint of the history of religions, the warrior, the *kshatriya*, is the one who struggles with the forces of chaos in order to maintain cosmic order. The modern mystique of the military corps, living still, with its music, uniforms, and parades, is a leftover of a faith like that. The warrior is the nobleman, the knight, the representative of power in the service of authority. But the authority came from God.[9] The warrior is the guardian of the order of the universe, the guardian of peace. The belief that a country's military personnel are its warranty for peace can still be discerned at the inmost heart of those who oppose the pacifists and those who advocate the disappearance of the army as an institution. It is forgotten that the modern way of making war has nothing in common with the chivalry of old.[10] Until now, tradition had held. Nowadays things have changed.

PEACE AS A POLITICAL PROBLEM

Political peace, by contrast, had little in common with "religious peace." And this despite the fact that there had been sporadic theoretical religious speculation concerning peace.[11]

Generally speaking, the established religions were in agreement with the political status quo. And understandably enough.

After all, they lived in it, if not on it. The political status quo was questioned only very rarely, and scarcely constituted a problem for religions. Peace consisted, simply, in the absence of war.[12]

Religious peace, on the other hand, was regarded more as an inner attitude, a personal tranquillity, a moral power, a condition of the soul. And this despite the fact that many words like *salām, shanti, shalom, eirēnē, pax,* and *mir*[13] originally had a political and a religious meaning at once.

These concepts accentuate rather the whole character, spiritual and material, of human peace (by contrast with an exclusively spiritualistic or only political sense). But an awareness of the intrinsic connection between the spiritual and the material has been all but lost in the West. And it has been weakened in the rest of the world as well, since the centuries of Europe's political sovereignty.[14]

The modern religious bibliography on the subject of peace speaks of peace as a gift of the Holy Spirit, or as the result of some enlightenment or actual vision.[15]

Pax aeterna is an eschatological concept; and *pax animae* is an ascetical notion.[16] *Pax* also has, naturally, a moral character, and a certain social aspect, since it also means "concord."[17]

The true religious peace is the *pax spiritualis.*[18] The *pax temporalis,* by contrast, belongs to an inferior degree, and, frequently, is set in opposition to genuine peace. After all, what will it profit the rich or mighty person to possess all things, if that person will have to suffer for it eternally?[19]

To say it another way: There is a political peace and a religious peace. The same word covers two spheres that are frequently very different: the spiritual or religious sphere, and the political or secular sphere. The latter indicates rather *securitas, tranquillitas, iustitia, unitas, concordia,* and, also, *utilitas.* Here it is a matter not of a *pax spiritualis,* but of a *pax civilis.*[20]

One explanation of this state of affairs might be the following: political war robs persons of their tranquillity, and accordingly, requires them to take a position with regard to the ultimate human questions. It requires, when all is said and done, that they make a religious response. On the other hand, political peace, in the best of cases, is a mere condition for the genuine internal peace of the person. True, political peace cannot be dispensed with, and is always advantageous for the peace of the soul. But it is the latter, ultimately, that counts. Political peace is perceived simply as the status quo. Its maintenance is precisely the task of the politicians, and not that of religion.[21] This is what was generally thought.

32

This state of things in the christian West might be regarded as a reaction to the conception of peace prevailing in judaism, according to the Bible, and which was also that of the christian Middle Ages.[22]

A concern for peace usually has a special tendency to appear in times of crisis.[23] And this is indeed what is occurring at the present time.[24]

THESIS

Our thesis[25] consists of two parts and a corollary: (1) Peace is an eminently religious affair. (2) The journey to peace requires interculturality, not as an academic luxury, but as an exigency of *lèse-humanité* (it requires what I have called cultural disarmament). (3) Postmodernity stands in need of a *metanoia*. Let us try to formulate all of this.

Religious Dimension

As we have observed, political war has always come upon the scene as a religious phenomenon, while modern political peace, up until now, has not been regarded as bound up with particularly religious problems. The *pax civilis* has been ruled by other laws than has the *pax spiritualis*.

The thesis of this book attempts to overcome this mortal dichotomy, and is the following:

Secularity, as a *novum* of our times, enables us to discover the religious dimension of political peace, without thereby falling victim to any theocracy. The *pax civilis* is the indispensable constituent of the *pax religiosa*, and vice versa.

This thesis attempts to overcome dualism, but without falling into monism. It is a nondualistic thesis.[26]

It goes without saying that the very concept of "religion" must be purified, possibly transformed, and, of course, purged of the predominantly institutional tone of its usual western key. It ought to denote the religious dimension of Man, which the various religious traditions express in different ways.

If I ask myself what is the interest of calling this profound aspect of peace "religious," I should adduce two reasons. *First:* Because it is this dimension of ultimacy that characterizes religion. And ultimacy, in the case before us, is not only individual but social. It is a question of life or death not only for the individual but for society as well.[27] *Second:* Because religions, despite the multitude of excrescences that time, routine, and power have deposited on them, continue to function as the junction for a new restructuration of this dimension. The fact that religion must not be confused with an institution in no way militates against the appropriateness, and even, at times, the necessity, of institutions for human life.

Cultural Disarmament

By this somewhat mordant expression, we wish to refer to the necessary interculturality of a serious effort for peace. Not only is peace not the monopoly of any determinate culture—although there are more and less warlike cultures—but, further, the very concept of "peace" is not univocal. It has distinct meanings, each in function of the various respective cultures. This is what we have meant by saying that peace is a symbol rather than a concept.

The expression "cultural disarmament" refers in a special way to the predominant culture, which has a scientific and technological character and is of European origin.[28] It is not a matter of depriving of their vitality the other cultures, which, generally speaking, suffer from an inferiority complex often accompanied by a real inferiority, although of course the latter concept is relative to a determinate scale of values.

By "cultural disarmament" I understand the abandonment of the trenches in which "modern" culture, of western origin, has dug in, regarding its values as vested and nonnegotiable, such as progress, technology, science, democracy, and the world economic market, not to mention governmental organizations. It is easy to see, then, that the expression is not malapropos. Disarmament makes a person vulnerable, and must be reduced to reality gradually; but it is a necessary condition for the establishment of a dialogue on an equal footing with the other cultures of the earth. One must realize that dialogue, concerning which so much is presumed, is utterly impossible without conditions of equality. Indeed, it is insulting to speak of dialogue to someone who is starving to death, or has been stripped of all human dignity, or who does not even know what we are talking about because his or her suffering or difference in culture generates an incapacity for doing so.

It will be well to insist on this point. By "cultural disarmament," or the "disarmament of modern culture," I mean to allude to a radical change in the predominant myth of contemporary humanity—of that part of humanity that is most vociferous, influential, and wealthy, and is in control of the destinies of politics. This work is not the task of a given period, nor is it even of a historical kind. Our frame of reference is not the politics reflected in the media, nor even concrete historical awareness, since what is at stake is the very myth of history.[29] It might be thought that what I propose is a utopia. This may be. But, aside from its value as a utopia, in this case one must reflect that the alternative is human, planetary catastrophe.[30]

In saying that we refer preferentially to the predominant culture, we meant to indicate that cultural disarmament also refers to the cultural project of the historical Man, as we shall see below. Today is not the first time that peace has been threatened.

Cultural disarmament calls for the abandonment of evolutionism as a form of thought—a mindset that goes far beyond "scientific evolutionism," a topic that we shall not address here. Evolutionism as a way of thinking implies, on one hand, the belief that a knowledge of the chronological genesis of a fact is synonymous with its intelligibility. On the other hand, it imples that the history of humanity, despite its manifold meanderings, has followed a linear evolution. And I say "history," because we are questioning not a possible human evolution from the paleolithic age to the neolithic, but the historical (and not prehistoric) evolution in which an evolutionary line seems to appear, from the Babylonians, Egyptians, Chinese, and Indians, through the Greeks, Romans, medievals, and moderns, peaking in contemporary *homo technologicus,* to whom our thesis of cultural disarmament is being applied.

Corollary: Demythologization

If we are sincere in our "intercultural dialogue," and not merely tolerating other cultures as "folklore" for our entertainment and the solace of those who cannot attain to our degree of "development"; if we consider other cultures on a plane of equality, however relative: then we can no longer regard the "modern" myth as the necessary condition for dialogue and the fecundation of cultures, or for the discovery of a lasting peace for humanity, some 70 percent of which lives in conditions of concrete inferiority.[31]

It is not a matter, then, of seeking a "sustainable development."[32] It is a matter, rather, of subjecting to a critique the very notion of "development."[33] It is a matter not of "adequate technological comfort," but of a critique of current technoscience.[34] By "critique" we do not mean "destruction," or "reform," but the subjection of the myths of this culture to an intellectual demythologization. It is a hopeful sign that the number of voices that now reject the very idea of "development" as cultural colonialism is on the rise.[35]

Now, this cannot be done monoculturally.[36] No one is fully aware of his or her own myth. In order to recognize our own myth, we need the contribution of other cultures. And to this end we must

35

see our neighbor not only as some*thing* else, but as an *alius/alia,* some*one* else—not only as an object of observation or cognition, but as another source of intelligibility, and an independent subject of our categories. This is the basis of pluralism.[37] Dialogue is necessary for pluralism; but dialogue is possible, as we have said, only in conditions of equality. And these conditions cannot be realized without the cultural disarmament to which we have referred.

As we shall indicate below, cultural disarmament requires the demythologization of modern science, both as a universal science, and as the matrix in which the fecundation of which we are speaking must be realized. "Disarmament" means not the negation of our own values, but the non-utilization of those values as weapons for invasion with the excuse that it is the natives themselves who seek entry into the technocratic club.

We must be aware, furthermore, that this demythologization is, as a matter of fact, a remythologization.[38] We cannot eliminate myth. What we are doing is adopting another myth that seems to us more adequate for an understanding of the new situation. Hence the senselessness of absolutism. We are all dependent on the myth that envelops us, in which we obtain a certain understanding of our place in the world.

5 Political and Religious Peace

Actually, discussions on peace are old. But in the contemporary age, new aspects and new applications have been found.[1] The situation is different; and philosophical reflection, accordingly, is different as well. Human knowledge, too, is also situated in time and space.

The whole of humanity has never lived under a threat as universal as is the current menace. The coordinates of peace have changed.[2] It goes without saying that the framework of our considerations is not the European situation, but the world situation. Nor let us forget that the paradox I have dared formulate as a law prevailing in the current situation constantly receives further confirmation: that to all progress on the microsociological level, there corresponds a retreat in the macrosociological order. In a closed system, the growth of wealth on one side is counterbalanced by poverty on the other. The reason is plain: with natural rhythms broken by acceleration, and the whole earth transformed into a single system, only the "national economy" makes any progress, at the expense of progress anywhere else. And this includes the phenomenon of inflation.[3] All this has to do with peace.

The *pax civilis* is not only threatened by tyrants, dictators, emperors, or demagogues of every type. These have always existed. But previously it was possible to discover the true or supposed cause of the disorder, and to combat it.[4] Today, peace sees itself threatened by the system itself. The anonymity of the system, and the absence of a viable alternative, make the threat more dangerous. Modern Man feels threatened by external circumstances. We need only consider prevailing human inequalities, frightful injustices, or individual, social, and political insecurity, things that have not improved in the last thirty years.[5] We need only think of economic instability, the arms race, and so forth.[6]

The human being is also threatened internationally. The work ethos of the modern person—that is, the ideology of labor—and the society called for by the current technocratic complex leave neither time nor space for peace.[7] Consumerism, competition, a craving for notoriety, the need for growth (either grow or go bankrupt), the cult of novelty, the information bombardment that overwhelms our very perception, let alone our assimilation, may be key words here for describing our current state, which does not permit peace, although everything comes wrapped in euphemisms (like "business competition").[8]

In sum, peace has become problematic, precisely because it has become unstable and dubious. It is thought impossible to find a way out of the situation in which we find ourselves. How can we go backward? Neither would the problems be solved if the Americans or the Russians dominated the world. The problem goes far deeper than that.[9] It is no coincidence that, with the elimination of the Russian counterpoise, the world has seen the most sophisticated war, and the largest number of verbal "allies," in all history.[10]

In other words, the factual situation of the modern world forces us to reflect seriously on the problem, theoretical as well as practical, of peace and the means of attaining it.[11]

It is the practical situation in which humanity finds itself that determines the problem and shapes its outline. If peace is so much spoken of today, it is because it cannot be regarded as something obvious. The old discussion about whether peace was something natural—because the human being is a kindly animal—or a cultural product in need of cultivation (an "instituted" thing) has been practically forgotten in our day.[12] The contemporary problem of peace is new, and the current situation is so complicated that any considerations on whether it is or is not "pure nature" awakens little interest. The urgent banishes the important. The possible destruction of the human race, or a great part of it—which, according to some, is actually probable—represents a *novum* in the history of human awareness. This perspective of a sociology of knowledge could indeed offer a foundation for what we seek to express in this study. Concepts like those of the *pax perpetua* of the theologians and philosophers, or the *pax romana, britannica, americana,* or the *pax socialista* of the politicians, have ceased to be operative notions in the greater part of the world. Now it is a matter of the problem of terror, with the possibility of thermonuclear destruction.[13] The atom—the indivisible—is split, and with it, peace.[14]

It seems no longer possible to address the problem of peace peacefully. One approaches it with anguish and trembling. How can we speak of peace in Nicaragua, in Ethiopia, in the Middle East, in Kampuchea, and so on? And many fear that the situation could grow still worse. This coefficient of danger, of threat, of not knowing what to do, of powerlessness, and, at the same time, of urgency, must be kept in account in order to understand and appraise considerations of peace in our days. Peace is more than a merely academic problem. As long ago as the year 44 of our era, Cicero asked Cassius: "Quod enim est, quod contra vim sine vi fieri possit?" (What is there that can be done against force without force?) To which the appropriate answer would be to introduce the subtle, delicate distinction between "force" and "violence."

Authentic theory arises from experience based on praxis. And hope, which is expressed in theory, also affects the practical situation.[15] This is not the moment to address this problem—which, since Pythagoras, joins *theōria, praxis,* and *therapeia;*[16] which, since the *Dhammapāda,* reminds us that word is sterile, beautiful though it be, unless one acts in accordance with it;[17] which, since Atīśa, tells us, recalling Vimalakīrti, that "theory without praxis is slavery."[18] It was not Marx but Francis of Assisi who said, "Tanto un uomo sa, quanto fa" (One knows as much as one does).[19] An authentic meditation on peace must not be only peaceful; it must be also pacifying.

This manner of considering the problem of peace is decisive for a sociology of knowledge.[20] We do not think in a vacuum. The very historicity of the human being inclines us to suppose that we are nearing the end of history, which does not mean that the end of the human being is drawing near.[21] Man as historical consciousness is approaching his end, with a nuclear catastrophe or without.[22]

INTERCULTURAL REFLECTION

The existential urgency of the subject inclines me to depart somewhat from the intercultural state of the question, important as it is, and so dear to our hearts.

In order to speak of peace, we should have to keep account of other cultures, and their ideas on the same. The West is not alone in this world. Nor is peace an exclusively western concept. But this would lead us too far afield, since the problem of peace is formulated in different worlds and in different ways.[23] In a large part of the East, for example, either there is no separation between politics and religion, or else the two concepts head in different directions because they correspond to different categories. In order to enter into this problematic we should have to apply new categories; accordingly, the first thing we should have to do would be to establish the identity of these categories and explain them.[24] We cannot undertake this now. However, the world situation is such that what is at stake is the "To be or not to be"—formulated centuries before Shakespeare as *astitinastiti*[25]—which requires the collaboration of all cultures. The solution to the problems of the world is not to be sought within one culture, nor will it be possible to find it monoculturally. Let us realize that not even the questions are the same. But the expansion of the western system across the face of the earth bestows a character of priority on the western state of the question. And this is all the more the case inasmuch as, for the moment, there seems to be, de facto, no other alternative. Therefore we are limiting ourselves in this study to what I call "cultural disarmament." Only in a second phase shall we be able to introduce certain intercultural considerations.[26] For the moment, let us try to achieve a certain degree of clarity vis-à-vis the western situation.

Definition of Concepts

Many of the concepts that we employ in this study are found to be charged with such diverse content that, frequently, they become mere analogies of one another. Thus, we here indicate the sense in which we use these words.

1. By *politics* I understand the aggregate of principles, symbols, ideas, means, and activities (all of them generally, though not exclusively, crystallized in institutions) by which human beings strive to achieve the common good (*bonum commune*) of the *polis*. The common good is interpreted here as the achievement of human plenitude within social life.[27]
2. By *religion* I understand the aggregate of principles, symbols, ideas, means, and activities (all of them generally, though not exclusively, crystallized in institutions) by which human beings believe that they achieve the supreme good (*summum bonum*) of *life*. This supreme good is interpreted here as the achievement of maximal plenitude within the life of all reality.

The concepts used to explain these two words actually ought

to be set in quotation marks. For example, it might be that the "supreme good" would be precisely the discovery that there is no such thing, and that "plenitude" could be nothingness.[28]

In the usual interpretation, these two words, "religion" and "politics," are understood, respectively, as the bond (*religio*, from *religatio*) between the human being and transcendence (*religatio divina*); and the bond of human beings with one another (*religatio humana*). If the former—religion—were to represent the vertical dimension of human existence, the latter—politics—would represent the horizontal dimension. Thus, religion would constitute the area of the sacred, the supernatural, the eternal; politics would represent the space of the profane, the natural, the temporal.

My intention, in this study, is to transcend this interpretative dualism that I have called the "usual" interpretation of both words.

3. By *peace* I understand the synthesis of three primordial experiences of the human being, which would be: harmony, freedom, and justice, as I shall explain in Part 3 of this study.[29]

The concept of "peace" does not indicate a passive state. The word denotes activity and dynamic relation. The celebrated *tranquillitas ordinis*,[30] which has colored the western concept of "peace" since the Stoics—through Augustine—has contributed to something of an undermining of the relational and dynamic aspect implied by peace.[31]

That peace has to do with security and love (*minne—caritas*) is abundantly attested in the history of the West.[32] We shall develop this notion further below. For the moment, suffice it to say what we have said thus far.

4. By *political peace* I understand the result of an order that makes the human being's fullness possible in human society, in the *polis*.[33]

5. By *religious peace* I understand the result of an order that makes the human being's fullness possible in the whole of reality.

In these last two cases, we find peace as a condition, as a necessary space, for the development of human possibilities. Peace is not identified with human perfection here. Peace is rather that relationship prevailing among human beings that enables perfection, felicity, or, to use another word whose denotation has been unduly narrowed in the common language, *salvation* (liberation, wholeness, fullness, *sōtēria, mokṣa, nirvāṇa, tao*). Peace is *cosmotheandric harmony*.[34]

6 Religious Transformation of Political Peace

TRADITION

"Chassez la nature, elle revient au galop" (Evict nature, back she comes on the double).[1] Exile the human being's religious instinct to the sphere of the supernatural, the eternal, or to the private life of the individual, and you force it to return, in a hundred different, not always wholesome, ways, to the agora of political and social life, not excluding the economic.

Actually these pages are an attempt to develop just one consequence of a more general conception when it comes to religion and politics.[2]

On one hand, an identification of religion with politics represents a monistic view of reality. Herein every type of theocracy, caesaropapism, and dictatorship receives its support, whether it be on the religious side or the political. On the other hand, a separation between "politics" and "religion" represents a dualistic view of reality, and hereon rest the superficial anarchisms and pragmatisms. And this is as true when religion is reduced to the individual and private sector (the saving of souls for a future life) as when politics is reduced to a selection of the most effective means to the attainment of an end already fixed and no longer under discussion. Religion is more than a technique for finding the road to heaven, and politics is more than a technique for using means. Roads to what heaven? Means to what ends?

If we ask about the ends and meaning of that which is human, and consequently of the present life as well, it is impossible to separate religion from politics so neatly.

The authentic relation between religion and politics—a relation corresponding to the nature of both, founded on the essence of the human being, and, in the last analysis, grounded in the very structure of reality—is a nondualistic relation. Temporal problems are also religious ones. Considerations on the end of the human being are political ones as well. The political cannot exist in separation from religion. There is no religious act that is not also, at the same time, political. All of the great human problems of today are of a political, and at the same time, of a religious nature: hunger, justice, lifestyle, paneconomic culture, capitalism, socialism, and so on. Peace constitutes a typical case, and proves the truth of this assertion.

After a period of human history in which religion impregnated the whole of it indiscriminately, there came a stage of clarification and differentiation, culminating in the extreme modern individualism of the West. The religious element, according to this last conception, has to do with the beyond, the supernatural, the divine, the transcendent, *nirvāṇa*, *pāramārthika*, eternity, and with the inscrutable interior.

The profane, on the other hand, is made up of this life, *vyāvahārika,* the natural, the human aspects of existence, politics, the external, temporality, and so forth. Neither sphere has anything to do with the other. They ought simply to respect each other. But human life does not permit this *apartheid.* The place where the twain meet is history, which is where the human being's destiny is played out. But in this field, peace does not reign. War prevails instead. "Militia est hominis vita super terram."[3] *Pax temporalis* is only *pax imperfecta.*[4] In the Bhagavad Gītā, Arjuna must hear and learn from Krishna that the temporal order is mere appearance.[5] The holy indifference of so many eastern and western spiritualities is self-sealing, since, from start to finish, there is no difference between doing one thing or doing another in the sphere of the profane. Each yields the same result. Nothing has any importance. Everything is indifferent—equidistant from eternal life, which is the only true life.

The fact that earthly things have no impact on the religious destiny of human beings gave religions a sovereign independence vis-à-vis profane regimes. On one hand, religions could support and bless just wars (and even participate in them). Disturbing a peace like political peace, which was so imperfect, had no very great importance, because true *pax perpetua*[6] was not in question. On the other hand, these same religions were able to detach themselves from temporal affairs and leave the avatars of peace to the responsibility of the politicians, to the "secular arm," as—in a revealing expression—the Tribunals of the Inquisition did. The religious sphere was regarded as worlds apart from politics, provided the latter "respected the rights" of the former. Peace as *pax civilis* was not a religious problem. For example, let christians vote for any political party they wish. The church does not meddle in politics, provided the church is permitted to exercise its rights. But who decrees what those rights are? And so it comes about that lay christians are customarily regarded by secular governments as a kind of fifth column. Christians read in the Bible, "Et mundum tradidit dispositioni eorum."[7] Their reign is not of this world.[8] But "la politique des domaines séparés" is not feasible.

Lest anyone take scandal—which we ought not to call "pharisaical," since the Pharisees, generally speaking, were honorable folk—at the hypocritical practices of christendom, we might well recall the growing governmental practice of maintaining official secret organizations (called "intelligence services" or "security services") that function with full autonomy—that is, utilizing any and every means—at the service of governments whose heads do not "stoop" to inquiring into the details of how "information" is obtained. Amnesty International's denunciations are sparing. Peace bears on all of this.

That this state of affairs is still operative could be seen in the relatively recent Malvinas (Falkland) Islands conflict. Although Pope John Paul II clearly and unequivocally pronounced himself in favor of peace, and even summoned the bishops of Great Britain and Argentina to Rome, the joint declarations of the two episcopates in Rome consisted merely in vague commonplaces about peace; and when they returned home, both bodies defended the nationalistic positions of their respective homelands, or at any rate did not condemn them.[9] The same can be said of the behavior of religious authorities on the occasion of the Gulf War: while the Pope unequivocally condemned the war, even the Italian bishops used another, much more ambiguous, language.[10]

Those distinctions of the last century still prevail in traditional circles: separation of church and state; an "impartial" attitude on the part of the churches, which ought not to meddle in temporal matters; separation between the temporal and the eternal, between this life and the life beyond, between the political lot of peoples and their religious salvation; the distinction between reason and faith, between clergy and laity, and so on. And as in so many other matters, the West delivered itself from the regime of christendom by going to the opposite extreme.

In this respect, politics had one finality: to facilitate and guarantee religious freedom, in such a way that the individual might be able to practice his or her piety privately. This privatization of religion went to the point that, for example, in the same catholic church, some folk were blessing German tanks while others blessed French cannons. And each faction could celebrate Mass for the victory of its respective people. The state should only guarantee freedom of religious practice. Today's situation in Latin American is meaningful: the churches have all the freedom they desire, so long as they do not interfere in "political" questions. The jurisdiction of the church is respected to the precise extent that it hold its tongue on matters referring to the *civitas hominis,* that is, precisely to the extent that it allow the state full liberty. Let Pius XII not meddle in Nazi affairs, nor American christian hierarchs denounce the CIA!

Pax, understood here as *pax civitatis,* the guardian of security and order, is simply the office of the politicians, and ultimately of the police. Accordingly, "political peace" would not be a religious category. It would be, at the most, a useful condition. "Peace" is the peace of the state, said Bodin.[11] Or, to paraphrase Hobbes: "Auctoritas, non veritas facit pacem."[12] "Recht ist Friede," wrote Fichte.[13] In none of this is there so much as a trace of religion.

It ought to be clear enough that there is no question of returning to theocratic regimes, or of christendom; that it is not a matter of falling anew into heteronomy. This is not the alternative to the autonomy that we now criticize. What is to be sought is *ontonomy:* the constitutive relation that unites the diverse poles of one and the same reality.[14] You don't have to throw the baby out with the bathwater.

That this state of things can no longer be supported is evident in our days. The "Century of Lights" firmly believed that "die Vernunft fordert Frieden" (reason fosters peace), as Carl von Rotteck wrote in 1838.[15] But Kant's pure reason and practical reason have shown themselves to be impotent. Factual conflicts are too real and too frequent. Theoretical problems are too palpable. Modernity has introduced a change in mentality. We have lost rational innocence, which believed that "vivere secundum rationem" (living according to reason), came down to "vivere secundum naturam," and that "natura," in turn, was simply "natura naturata" (created nature).

THREE FACTORS OF MODERNITY

Western modernity can be defined in many different ways, but there are three basic factors whose presence is undeniable: *technocracy,* which has now advanced so far that it has split the atom;

secularity, which has penetrated religion itself; and the *primacy of history,* which has managed to monopolize life. The combination of these three factors has decisive consequences for our subject. It stations peace at the center of human awareness, and transforms it into a religious reality of the first order, without thereby attenuating its political character.

Technocracy

As we confront this enormous problem, we must especially take account of the fact that technocracy constitutes a world in itself.[16]

The first difficulty is terminological. When there are no adequate words to formulate a problem, that means not only that the question is difficult and delicate, but that the reality struggling to come to adequate expression has not yet wholly reached the light of day in the realm of a determinate culture.

My hypothesis maintains that there is a qualitative leap between technics, understood as the Greek *technē*, and modern technology. The former represents a human invariable. All peoples have *technē,* art, artifacts, the manipulation of nature, elementary or first-degree machines, the mentality of arts and crafts. Perhaps the most adequate term for this reality would be "craftsmanship," whose human space is the cultural organism: agriculture and techniculture. All peoples have craftsmanship. Culture is craftsmanship. Modern technology, however, is the fruit of one civilization, and it bears its marks about with it wherever it goes, even when it is "the natives" who introduce it into their respective cultures with a "Trojan horse." (We shall say something about this in Part 3.) Modern technology's human space is rational organization: technocracy.[17]

As the latter—technology—is sprung (albeit by mutation) from the former—technics—therefore the West has not changed the root of the name. Hence the difficulty in distinguishing them. Hence also the fact that both are commonly called "technology." The identification seems all the more plausible by reason of the evolutionistic and progressivistic mentality with which the modern West has attempted to justify, consciously and unconsciously, its world domination: all is evolutionary progress, from the Stone Age to our western civilization. From fire to electricity, arrows to nuclear missiles, a linear, homogeneous (with peaks and valleys, of course) evolution mounts to the sky. This progress can of course be used for good or evil—as if good and evil were values fallen from the sky independently of precisely the ideology that seeks to justify these values. As we have said, evolutionism is the mental attitude that thinks it can reach intelligibility (of a state of things) by uncovering the temporal genesis of the phenomenon in question. And so, we hear, a nuclear missile launcher is only a (sophisticated, of course) extension of the technique of the slingshot, joined to the accelerated phenomenon of the sprouting of a seed.

We shall not go into this topic, but shall limit ourselves to a consideration of the terminology involved. To call the former "technics" and the latter "technology" has the drawback of seeming to reduce the former to a naive primitivism, and of excluding from the word "technology" the meaning of "study of technics." And so I call "technology" by the name of "technocracy," based on the etymology of the word and the fact that, unlike technics, technology is not a mere first-degree tool, to be wielded at the pleasure of the consumer, but requires and imposes a way of thinking, and a lifestyle, and can exist only in this "fourth world" that I have called the "artificial," and which it would be better to call, simply, the "mechanical." Technocracy represents the step from *technē* as art, as craftsmanship, to technics as dominion, as *kratos*, as power.

Lest we interrupt our discourse, we shall present a certain number of considerations on technocracy from one viewpoint only: that of time.

Technocracy has a time of its own, which is neither nature's, nor that of the temporality—the historicity—of culture. Technocracy's time is *technochrony*, and is based on acceleration.[18] Human beings must adapt to this acceleration if they hope to survive in the technocratic world. The self-sufficiency of technocracy—which, of course, is more than applied natural science, inasmuch as it implies an entire civilization—reaches its culmination in "nuclear energy," which is the unleashing, that is, the accelerated expansion, of the energy stored in the atom.[19] This acceleration of energy creates the possibility, or even, some would say, the probability, of the extermination of the human species.[20]

And the likelihood in question is based not only on the fact that one or several individuals might actually decide to cause this extermination, but also on the theory of probability as applied to the system itself.[21]

To put it in traditional terms: suicide represents the radical negative response to the loss of all personal hope; and the temptation to suicide comports the fostering of that possibility. This individual syndrome is now converted into a collective one. Humanity itself contemplates this possibility, and the proof is that it assumes the risk. A God who permits the annihilation of the human race, the very work of the divine hands, becomes daily less worthy of credit, that is true.[22] But a self-destructive human race is even less worthy of credit. Faith in humanity, which, for so many, had replaced faith in God, is also on the wane. Men are ceasing to believe in the Man. The simple people of the West suffer, and are demoralized. How, for example, shall they ever accept a wage-adjustment policy when they know the wastefulness of the arms race? Peace, the human order, the fertility of mother earth, and all the rest—in sum, life and its flowering on this planet—are called into question, and not only metaphysically (Why is there being instead of nothingness?), but physically, sociologically, and even psychologically, as well. (Why are we squandering the earth and destroying ourselves? Why can we not stop cooperating with the growing destruction of humanity and the planet?) Peace no longer depends on the will of God, or of a certain number of persons. It is as if it were simply "up in the air." It depends on no one. Does it depend on chance, or on good or bad luck?

A kind of blind fatality weighs on human beings. There is no one of whom to beg mercy—the grace of peace, as the *Rig Veda* (X, 121, 1d, 2d, and passim) prophetically foretold. What God can we invoke? To whom can we direct our pleas? The system is anonymous. For example, everyone wants to hold down inflation (at least, simple people think that everyone does); there is no lack of goodwill; and yet, no one manages to do so. All the world wants peace, and it seems to slip through everyone's fingers. And then we hear of drugs, or alcoholism, or depression—the list is endless, and the situation is the same.

The belligerents of World War II have never signed a peace treaty. So the war is not over. And indeed, the 145 wars that have taken place in the world since 1945 have taken the lives of more persons than the entire Second World War. And the process goes on unstoppably.[23]

I have denominated the aspect of time's domination by technocracy, "technochrony." Technochrony is the time proper to second-degree machines, to technocracy. Accordingly, it is the time proper to the modern city. Therefore I have contradistinguished "cultural organism" (technics) from "technocratic organization." The time in question is one of *acceleration*.[24]

Once that time is accelerated in which Man sees himself forced to live in order to subsist in technocratic civilization, that acceleration can no longer be reduced without causing disturbances in the Man, in society, in the city, and even in the earth, all of which may see themselves teetering on the brink of out-and-out catastrophe. We need only think, for example, of the basic question of nutrition.

A restoration, in the sense of a romantic return to the preindustrial, pretechnocratic age, is almost unthinkable, much less practicable. Once natural rhythms are broken, their restoration is not easy, since life's capacity for adaptation has already assimilated a great part of the arrhythmia in question. Once the human being has become habituated to monocultures, pharmaceutical products, or national boundaries, their dismantling is a very delicate operation. Therefore the process must be not a negative or violent one, but one of emancipation.[25]

On the other hand, if the acceleration—in this age of the machine—continues to grow unabated, it will be more and more impossible to stop. Grow or die, we are told. But there seems to be no appreciation of the fact that rampant growth means cancer, in all orders.[26]

The economic example is manifest. The industrialized world lives face to face with the future embracing the hypothesis that growth and progress will always be possible. Capital, which has now become necessary for everything, has mortgaged its tottering future. The average American citizen has already spent three years' wages in advance: that is, has mortgaged them. In order to grow a few acres of rice scientifically, fifteen times more unrecoverable energy must be put into them than the number of calories the finest harvest will make available from that acreage. And this "scientific" rice is sold on the (free?) market for a "better" price than rice grown at a natural rate.[27] Who pays for this? All of this has to do with peace. Peace can no longer be regarded as the preservation of the status quo: first, because this status quo is unstable; and second, especially because it is unjust.

This view of things could be interpreted as a kind of attenuated apocalypticism, were it not for the fact of the second *novum* of modernity: secularity. But it is not our intent to send up a millenarianistic smoke screen.

Secularity

Another complex, difficult question is constituted by secularity.[28] I shall limit myself exclusively to distinguishing among three notions: secularization, secularism, and secularity.

"Secularization" denotes the familiar process, especially in European history, of the confiscation of the properties of the church and religious institutions, with all the implications of that process in terms of anticlericalism, deistic humanism, and so on.

"Secularism" is an ideology that asserts that religion, as a flight to transcendency, must be abolished as anachronistic, antiscientific superstition. The process of its elimination can be implemented either in a revolutionary fashion, or else gradually, by means of the state or through education.

"Secularity," on the other hand, represents the modern Man's belief—which can perhaps be regarded as a trickle-down from various movements—in the definitive, and therefore irreducible, character of the *saeculum*.

The *saeculum* is the triad of time, space, and matter, which, in its intimate oneness with human life, constitutes an irrevocable, definitive dimension of reality. Whatever be its relationship with transcendency, the immanence of the *saeculum* is not transitory. The *saeculum* (*aiōn, aheu, āyus*) is the time interval, the duration, the temporal tension in which every living being, or at least the human being, lives and develops. This "space" pertains to the Man's very life, and has a meaning in itself. This *saeculum*, as the space of temporality, has a reality of its own, and cannot be regarded merely as an intermediate stage along the road to eternity and the "other world."[29] Secularity represents the defeat of Platonism.

"Secularity" means the experience of time (at least of human time, or temporality) as an ultimate and definitive, although not the single, component of reality. Neither is time a mere illusion, nor are time and eternity two distinct forms of reality. Rather, they are two inseparable dimensions of reality, in mutual and constitutive interpenetration. Consequently, secularity is not the antithesis of sacrality. The sacred and the profane are opposites; but the secular transcends this dichotomy, and a secular affair can be as sacred as any other affair conducted by the traditional religions.[30] It is precisely secularity that delivers the ancient religions from their temptation to deny—and abandon—the world and thus become nontranscendent for our time.[31] Mysticism, well understood, can help us understand the nondualistic experience of tempiternity.[32]

The Myth of History

Traditional Man, in most cultures, lives not in history, but in the cosmos.[33] His life is reflected not exclusively, or even mainly, in human history, but rather in the totality of cosmic forces. Men know that they are children of nature, and that they share in nature's lot. They come and they go, they are born and they perish. They belong to the universe, and only a small part of that same universe constitutes the historical development of their human fellows. For the traditional Man, generally speaking, the sun, or terrible suffering, or a harvest, or the numinous world (the will of God, for example), have

51

more meaning than does the "tribe" or the "nation" in their historical sense. By contrast, modern Man—and here is the connection with secularity and technocracy—lives in his historical environment, which constitutes the framework of his life. Each thing is dependent on its individual destiny. *Ṛta, physis, ordo,* and like notions, are reducible to human justice. Man is transformed into a historical being. "Reality," for him, is the same as "history," that is, what has occurred, is occurring, or will occur. History is the real; real is what occurs (historically, to be sure). Human existence is a historical existence. "Consciousness" is to know what is happening, has happened, or will happen. What would modern life be without science, or without news? Not only is Man a historical being; nature itself is historical.[34]

In a word, the "social order" is whatever Man has, unless he takes flight to a supernatural world or hides in his inner world. It is not a matter of indifference, then, how that social order unfolds *in se,* since it forms part of Man's very life and, consequently, of his happiness. The social status quo is all that Man possesses: if that framework is unjust, imperfect, or inhumane, he cannot survive. Man depends exclusively on his history. In this sense, peace among men becomes a matter of ultimacy, one on which all existence depends.

For a person of the ancient cultures, political circumstances did not have the ultimate, definitive character they have for the modern secular citizen. Strictly speaking, the very notion of "politics" was different.[35] Political peace was regarded as desirable and important, but the salvation of the Man did not depend on it. It may be that an intermediate situation, between the two, is closer to the reality of human existence; but the fact is that secular persons have the sensation that their salvation is in direct relation to their situation in the *polis.* This conviction immediately transforms political peace into a religious affair. From this perspective, Marx's criticism of religion as an antihistorical factor, which impedes the development of Man, is understandable. And the Marxist oversimplification of reducing history to a class struggle for control of the rudder of history can be grasped as well. But the consequences run deeper still. The binary digital system used in electronic recording, and so on, seems but the continuation to the point of outrage of the binary system of the Marxist class struggle converted into a class logic, with the classes reduced to two. It had been capital and labor, capitalists and workers. Now it is the maximal abstraction of one and two.

The misunderstanding—at times veritably tragic—between the Vatican and the theology of liberation is not due *solely* to political factors—factors of power—and doctrinal differences. It is due as well, and more fundamentally, to different lived experiences of the myth of history.

POLITICAL PEACE AS A RELIGIOUS PROBLEM

In political peace as a religious problem,[36] we have a sample of the change in religious awareness today: peace is rediscovering its religious roots. Thereby, not only does its study plunge to further depths, but the very concept of "religion" is purified, besides.[37] After the separation of religion and politics over the course of the last centuries, a nondualistic relationship presents itself once more as the only possible solution. Peace is no longer a simple *concordia civium*. The *pax civitatis* is no longer a simple *ordinata concordia*, nor a mere legal or purely intramundane term having little to do with religion, nor again a *pax temporalis apparens* or a *pax imperfecta*.[38] Instead, peace becomes a definitive, and therefore directly religious, matter. The reason is plain: the human being's welfare in the city of earth is no longer a purely provisional affair.[39] *Pax in terris* is a problem that concerns the entire being of human persons as such, since their final destiny is at stake in the *civitas hominis* itself. The city of earth is regarded no longer as simply a preparation for heaven, or as a reflection of the city of God, but as an arena in which Man's ultimate destiny is being forged. And this is the case regardless of whether the beyond is denied or affirmed.

The definitive destiny of the individual depends on what that individual has come to be in the realm of earth. Unless one has succeeded in attaining to the perfection of life to which one aspires, one will remain crippled forever.[40] Religion is not a consolation for the failed. Indeed, this realm is not merely temporal, but tempiternal, without there having to be any reason for a subsequent eternity. In other words, the political status quo is of immediate religious relevance, since it has directly to do with the definitive *status hominis*. To put it in very much oversimplified terms: if you do not believe in another life, what you actualize of life on earth becomes the ultimate and the definitive—becomes a religious matter; if you do believe in another life, its enjoyment in heaven will depend on what you have been on earth. If the earthly is a springboard to the heavenly, then earth also acquires definitive characteristics: the *pax terrena* that has enabled my perfection will acquire a religious importance as well.

To be sure, there can be no *pax* without *iustitia*. But neither can justice be split into "justification" for eternal life and "justice" for temporal existence. It is significant that the concept of christian *dikaiosynē* shifted further and further in the direction of justification

53

(for eternal salvation) and became separated from justice (among human beings).[41] The history of this split in western christianity encapsulates the whole problematic of our subject. The essence of justice consists not solely in *justitia socialis,* nor in mere *justificatio in vitam aeternam,* but rather in Man's authentic, complete relationship with reality. The essence of justice consists in the harmonious realization of all Man's constitutive relations. Justice is made up of the whole ensemble of Man's relations with all of reality. Persons cannot have a genuine relationship with God without at the same time entering into a harmonious relation with the cosmos, and especially with their fellows. Justice in its entirety, as a just order, is an essential ingredient of peace.

A concept that denounces this mortal division, which we are trying to heal, between the religious and the political is that of "salvation" (*mokṣa, sōtēria,* "liberation," *nirvāṇa*). This concept, in most religions, designates Man's full freedom, and thereby also his *salus,* that is, his fullness and happiness: freedom *from* all slavery, and freedom *for* all sovereignty. This human liberation gradually dissolved into (at least) three parts: a theological *salvation* for the future life, a medical *health* for the psychosomatic conjunct, and a *political freedom* for social life.

The grave consequence of all of this was not so much the specialization of the sciences as the dismemberment of Man.[42] What liberation theology seeks to do, in the concrete context of Latin America, is a good example of what I wish to express, although this example should not be transformed into a general model: the oppressed, conscious of the absence of justice, see therein a threat to their justification. That is, in their human marginalization and ostracism, they are at risk of eternal damnation. And vice versa: the powerful cannot be justified (saved) unless they comply with justice. The "bourgeois" criticism of the theology of liberation—that it has degenerated into a mere naturalism and political struggle—ignores the context in which that theology occurs: it has not heard the suffering cry of the poor, but has listened only to the threat to the lifestyle of the oppressors. Temporality, too, is the object of the theological undertaking. Mere "conscientization" (consciousness-raising)—as I have written elsewhere—leads not only to rebellion but to desperation, when the oppressed see not only that they cannot deliver themselves from their oppression but that neither can they deliver their children from it. One must have lived in contact with the oppressed in order to realize that, in becoming "conscientized," they come to notice that at stake is not only their human happiness but also their eternal salvation itself. They realize that misery has destroyed them—that they are no longer capable of human reactions; that they lack the knowledge, virtues, and habits that would be necessary in order to react in a fitting manner; that, really and truly, oppression has demeaned them to the level of brute beasts; and that they no longer even desire their liberation, since they scarcely know what they are—they have lost the taste for life. They have been oppressed to the very quick. The absence of justice has destroyed their capacity for justification. They no longer want it, or even know what it is. We must be extremely cautious with respect to glorifying the poor. The tragedy rests in the fact that marginalization attains its ends: it causes the marginalized to degenerate. It is understandable, then, that the cry of liberation theology should be more than a game of class struggle: it is the struggle for salvation.

Something of the like ought to be said about the relation between medical salvation (health) and religious salvation, on one side, and political on the other.[43]

The movement Religion for Peace, born in Kyoto in 1970 and embracing some dozen religions, may, along with its forerunners, be another sign of our times.[44] It was very meaningful to me to hear representatives of various religions frequently expressing themselves in direct opposition to their traditional doctrines. The struggle for human peace, that is, for a *pax civilis,* is not only a natural task, incumbent upon all of us as citizens, but also one having a certain religious priority in the current context.[45] These voices grow louder by the moment. It is instructive, for example, to hear and read interpretations of buddhist *nirvāṇa,* which set it in direct relation to believers' socioeconomic situation.[46]

Another astonishing manifestation of the new religious awareness was the UNESCO conference in Bangkok in 1979, at which representatives of eleven different religions met to investigate the problem of human rights in their respective traditions. Despite divergencies of philosophy and language, all participants were in agreement that sociopolitical rights were a religious object too, even though so little attention had been paid to it in the past.[47]

We need not recall here all the movements that have sprung up in this last decade, on religious initiatives, having the aim of showing the religious character of peace, and of defending at least a relative pacifism.[48] Let us cite only the Pax Christi movement, which is adopting more and more courageous positions.[49] It becomes ever more frankly understandable why a christian conscience should be incompatible with a collaboration with war industries and military power.[50]

Another example would be the encyclical *Pacem in Terris,* of John XXIII, whose very title is instructive. The Roman Pontiff speaks not of *pax in caelis,* but of earthly peace, to which he ascribes a religious transcendence. The encyclical accepts the sacrality of the secular sphere, in the sense of the secularity described above.[51]

If the human situation in the world has a religious meaning, that is, if it signifies something ultimate, then it is not without importance that Man should achieve the full development of his material or cultural, physical or economic life. This "full" refers, obviously, to each personal individual: it is a relative fullness, and is without an absolute sense. But it does not, for all that, fail to signify that salvation for human beings refers not only to their transcendent realization but also to their individual welfare, their family life, their social existence, and their creative activity in all spheres.

In a word, happiness, the *beatitudo* of the christian tradition, or India's *ānanda*, is not merely a beatitude to be experienced in the next life. Rather it is a tempiternal happiness, not exhausted in temporality, but neither located outside it. Eternal life is reflected in temporality. The real, concrete existence of human life is a tempiternal existence.

It is readily understandable, then, that, in this earthly peace, the ultimate, Man's eternal destiny, should be reflected. If human existence has not been perfected to the extent that it could have been—or rather, should have been—then this failure perdures, as an *abortus,* as a permanent "hole in reality." Christian tradition calls this abortion, this hole in reality, "hell" and warns that there is no returning from it.[52] Earthly failure is heavenly failure. *So in heaven as on earth.* Man's responsibility is little short of infinite, by virtue of the fact that human worth is an end in itself.

When more than forty years ago we heard of the dangers of the atomic bomb, our first reaction was concern and indignation. But the later reaction, in many representatives of the dualistic spirituality that I have been criticizing, was, in effect: "So what? Don't we know we're mortal? And not only as individuals, but as cultures, too, and as peoples? Aren't we aware that the solar system has already lived out half of its possible existence? What essential difference can there be between whether the world lasts only another hundred years or four-and-one-half billion years? Isn't this the law of life? What is any length of time, however great, in comparison with eternity? The human being's eternal element cannot be threatened or eliminated as easily as that."

But when the eternal element in the human being does not come *after* the temporal—since the two are inseparable—then all of those lives that have not been realized in time (*āyus, saeculum*), will likewise fail to find consolation in that religiousness of patience and ultraterrestrial compensation that have been proved so serviceable for the exploitation of others. Human life on earth is a game of life and death. The worth of the person is neither manipulable nor transferable.

Woe to those who oppress (scandalize) others, the Gospel tells us. And the curse is terrifying: it would have been better for them to have been drowned in the depths of the sea.[53]

When *kurukshetra* is at the same time *dharmakshetra*[54]—that is, when historical destiny finds itself inextricably interlaced with the final destiny of the person, when the salvation of the soul alone loses its meaning, then humanity's political, historical, and collective situation is no longer a secondary factor. Not that the temporal, the bodily, the sociopolitical exists by itself. But neither does the eternal, the spiritual, the theoretical exist without it.[55] Reality is indivisible.

There are not two cities.[56] The *homo religiosus* of our day no longer has a desire to be a citizen of two states. "No one can serve two masters."[57] It follows immediately that the citizenship of the religious human being cannot be satisfied with the modern megalopolis, which is built to the mere dimensions of a time and space reduced to mathematical abstractions. "On earth as it is in heaven," to be sure. But it is also true that "whatever you bind on earth will be bound in heaven"—whatever happens (whatever you bind) on earth will also be realized (bound) in heaven.[58] That is to say: *So in heaven as on earth*. Heaven and earth meet, indeed, merge, at the horizon. Only, that horizon is not merely in the future, nor simply in the *eschaton*, but is in the here and the now, when the latter are more than mere spatiotemporal categories. Presence is *parousia*.

God's peace and the world's peace can be neither identified nor separated. Their relation is nondualistic. There is no *post*-temporal eternity, nor any *pre*-eternal temporality. Reality is tempiternal.

In this sense, a peace that would afford security only to a few individuals, or that would offer a certain stability to only a few states, would be only that peace that catholic tradition has sometimes called a *pax imperata* or *pax violenta*.[59] It would be a *falsa pax*—or a *mala pax*, as Saint Augustine called it long ago[60]—since it would not fulfill the condition laid down by that same christian tradition: "Principium . . . pacis est, ad finem aeternum dirigere subditos" (The first principle of peace is to direct subjects to their eternal end).[61]

The novelty of secularity consists in this, that that *finis aeternus*

57

is not shifted or postponed to a life sovereignly independent of the earthly, in a heavenly beyond, but is realized precisely at the confluence of both currents of reality. This is the crossroads of the cross, and the meaning of the Incarnation. In any authentically religious horizon, heaven stoops to earth, and earth mounts to heaven. In other words, human existence itself is not only earthly but divine as well; not only spiritual but bodily as well; not only eternal but temporal as well. And all of this in a plenitude without either confusion or separation. This is the nondualistic (and Chalcedonian, we might add, for christians) relation.[62]

All of this must not be interpreted as if there were a question of a negation of the transcendent or of mystery. We defend no superficial humanism.[63] Neither is true peace temporal, nor does it consist in a purely eschatological eternity. It is neither spiritual and interior alone, nor political and social alone. There is no question of considering political peace to be a religious peace, as if the political dimension were identical with the religious.[64] Nor is it a matter of identifying religious peace with political peace. The function of religion is not only social: "Not on bread alone is man to live."[65] Human peace is not attained exclusively by satisfying the needs of the "rational animal," as if Man were but an ensemble of needs. Rather it is a matter of defeating, transcending, the dichotomy between politics and religion, without identifying them with each other. Actually there is no such thing as a peace that is purely political or purely religious. Human peace is political and religious at the same time— and this, precisely because it is human and Man is a totality.

Christians should have no great difficulty in accepting this when they consider that the Incarnation is not the exclusive privilege of the Son of Man, or if, following their own tradition, they believe in the *theosis* (divinization) of the human being, the doctrine that all the children of human beings are called to be children of God.[66]

The Upanishads' celebrated "correspondences" come down to the same thing.[67] A mutual relationship prevails between each and every person, considered as a microcosm, and the totality of the universe as macrocosm.[68] Or, as modern physics has rediscovered, every ultimate particle is actually a kind of field (magnetic, electrical, gravitational, atomic) in which every point is a function of all of the others, and in some sense a reflection of the totality of the field. Here we should refer to all of the modern works on *Gestalt, holism, holograms,* and so forth. Actually this is the ancient idea of the *triloka,* or notion of three worlds, alive in the East and West.[69]

What I should now like to emphasize is the mutual influence

between Man and the World where peace is concerned. Each person reflects the harmony of the universe, when this person is in his or her proper place, and is not alienated.[70] Thus, the cosmic harmony depends once more on the inner harmony of every being.[71] But an inward peace that were to be merely a private *pax spiritualis* would not really be "peace." Peace is not a parcel of private property. Peace is not only spiritual but bodily and social as well. Each of the two elements contributes in both directions—indeed, in the infinitude of directions of all beings: to the creation and preservation, as well as to the destruction, of the peace of the universe. What in jewish and christian spiritualities are known as "vicarious callings," whether for suffering, prayer, or action, corresponds in the buddhist or hindu context to *karma* and its micro- and macrocosmic equivalents. A saint inspired by love can surely do more for peace than an activist ruled by hatred.

To summarize: We have seen that the nuclear threat, the ecological situation, and social injustice have made modern Man aware of the fact that the status quo is not peaceful. Accordingly, peace cannot mean the preservation of that status quo. Secularity or the secular mentality, for its part, makes us conscious that the *fluxus quo* is a religious task, and consequently one that impels us to shape it. The combination of these two experiences thrusts us toward a change with regard to the human attitude toward peace. Religious peace and political peace intermingle. And this, not because either disappears into the other, but because a concrete separation between these two human spheres can no longer be maintained.

Peace, then, is neither the status quo nor the *fluxus quo,* but rather the mediation between them—that is, a kind of constant state of reconciliation. This does not mean that changes and revolutions are to be excluded.[72] This is the sore point, the point where the difficulty of peace stands to the fore. The step from status quo to *fluxus quo* must also be peaceful. Violence (not force) is to be excluded—understanding, by "violence," the violation of the person, or more broadly, the violation of the dignity of any being. Man has known since prehistoric times that it is more painful to extract an arrow than to drive it deeper. If the social body today is wounded by many arrows, there is nothing to be done but to withdraw them. And that is no easy task.

This step from political peace to religious peace reveals the place at which the tension between religion and politics becomes most visible.[73]

While a "realistic" political attitude is directed toward the attainment of peace—if always in terms of a conception based on the ancient principle, "Si vis pacem, para bellum" (If you would have peace, prepare for war)[74]—a genuinely religious posture asserts the vulnerability inherent in any authentic attitude in behalf of peace.[75] Concretely: disarmament projects have been mounted for some decades now. But they have met with no success, because their advocates have been laboring under an internal contradiction: they have not overcome the desire to create peace while preserving the status quo.[76]

Only in a true religious attitude do we find sufficient strength and responsibility to create a peace relatively free of conditions. The contrary attitude stimulates the coining of slogans like, "Better dead than red," "My country right or wrong," and similar watchwords, which leave no room for dialogue.[77]

For example, a religious attitude can decide in favor of unilateral disarmament, albeit a gradual one.[78] The religious attitude enables one to refuse to absolutize the "enemy." Thus, in the face of a threat of invasion by foreign troops, one can always discover that the loss of national liberty, for example, is not an absolute evil. The Spanish Civil War and World War II would offer us important considerations in this respect. Perhaps it would have been better not to resist with weapons. Peace is of its very essence antiwar.

A peace achieved under conditions imposed by only one of the parties is called "victory," but not "peace." Peace has an inner, religious substance; otherwise it is not peace. The peace of the world will not consist in the victory of one ideology alone—ours. Paradoxically, religion relativizes the demands of politics. A genuine religious spirit can attain to a certain human perfection even under a dictator, or under an unjust system. And this will leave one's hands free to transform oppressive systems into something more humane.

Part 3

Cultural Disarmament as Peace's Requirement

*Majoris est gloriae
ipsa bella verbo occidere
quam homines ferro;
et acquirere vel obtinere pacem pace,
non bello.*

It is more glorious a thing
to slay wars themselves with the word
than human beings with the sword;
and to win or keep peace with peace
than with war.

Augustine
Letter to Darius, 229, 2

Augustine writes this letter in his old age, a few years before his death, to the imperial envoy who is about to restore peace with the sword.

Peace would seem to belong to the realm of the unattainable. But the art of human life consists precisely in challenging the seemingly impossible. The more difficult of attainment anything seems to us to be, the greater the incentive to reach it for that being who is human by his participation in the creative act and who therefore has a thirst for the infinite. When parents simply tell their young children, "No, you can't have the moon," instead of pointing to a more real and more difficult moon than the one that they would like to have, they quench the human creativity that nestles in the breast of every little child.

Peace is not an adolescent's moon, it is the authentic moon of the Man that has not allowed himself to be reduced—or seduced—neither to the condition of a mere dreamer of something beyond the clouds nor to a simple calculator of the age of the firmament.

The subject of peace is a challenge to logic and to history. But neither logic nor history constitutes the whole of reality.[1]

Peace is not possible without disarmament. But the required disarmament is not only nuclear, military, or economic. There is also need for a cultural disarmament, a disarmament of the dominant culture, which threatens to become a monoculture capable of engulfing all other cultures and finally drowning along with them. Escaping to the moon or settling on Mars, besides being an alienation of Man's earthly body, would provide but a temporary refuge. Man is more than a bacterium that seeks merely to reproduce. Modern Man feels himself the prisoner of this earth, as some of their forebears felt themselves prisoners of their bodies, from which they only wished to escape. The "transfer" is significant and ironical. They no longer wish to go to heaven, but they do desire to go to the moon or other planets. They no longer believe in the starry vault of heaven, but they still believe in the stars as their heaven. Man was ill at ease in his body when he thought of it as just an envelope; now he feels uneasy on the earth when he thinks of earth as a simple apartment. And as once upon a time a bodily alienation reigned, now an earthly alienation is the order of the day. The consequences are our ecological disasters. Hence my cry for an *ecosophy*.

It is an all but immediate evidence that military disarmament is impossible without cultural disarmament. Within prevailing cultural parameters, military disarmament looks to be an improbable folly. Then will it be a balance of weaponry that will maintain the peace? But if one side disarms, the other will take advantage of it. Unless we keep making "progress" in the invention and development of deadly weapons, others will do so, and the balance will be thrown off. One must see who builds the biggest stockpile. The United States had built a bigger one than had the Soviet Union. The problem now is the next step.

We shall divide our topic into three chapters, each of which will be presented under three points. The first chapter will deal with *peace;* the second, with the *obstacles* in the way of peace; and the third, with *how it is to be acquired*. But none of them will consist of recipes.

7 Peace as Harmony, Freedom, and Justice

THE UNIFYING MYTH

Peace today constitutes one of the few positive symbols having meaning for the whole of humanity. Peace is the most universal unifying symbol possible. It is one of the few symbols to which the human race responds positively. God, who for some time had been the unifying symbol for many cultures, is no longer the center of human activities, at least in the cultures that revere the mechanistic organization of life. The symbol "God" has ceased to be universal—if it ever was—not only because of the wars that have been waged in the divine name, but also because, rightly or wrongly, a considerable part of human consciousness sees in the theisms the last residue of a monarchical conception of reality fated to disappear. But this is not our subject.[1]

Neither is a certain conception of democracy, or a certain economic welfare, a universal symbol. Man aspires to something more. Peace, however, seems to be something that all men, without distinction of ideology, religion, or personal disposition, accept as a positive, universal symbol. "Nemo est qui pacem habere nolit," wrote Saint Augustine (There is no one who does not wish to have peace).[2]

Symbols are the building blocks of myths. With a symbol, one can build many myths. By "myths," of course, we understand the horizons of intelligibility accepted by human beings and making possible the various *mythologoumena* lying at the basis of human cultures.[3]

63

A SIGN OF PEACE: HARMONY, FREEDOM, JUSTICE

What is peace? A very familiar emblem used to symbolize many movements for peace consists of a circle divided into three equal segments.

I shall use this sign without necessarily endorsing other uses that may be or have been made of it.

Peace is composed of three equal essential elements. To ignore any of them will necessarily deform its essence.

Harmony

Below, at the base, is *harmony*—the maximum value in Chinese culture, as it may be the minimum in current western culture, although it has been cultivated and loved in the West since the time of the Greeks. To say "harmony" is tantamount to saying "balance." It means not only *Ne quid nimis*[4] (Nothing to excess); it also means that each *quid* should have its place; that everything should be integrated; that nothing ought to be discarded: *ne quid futile*, even though, indeed, there may be something superfluous for us. There is no such thing as absolute evil. Harmony here is harmony between the inner and the outer, the body and the soul, the natural and the cultural, the masculine and the feminine, and so on—harmony among all sectors of reality. A goodly number of human cultures (the dualistic ones?) fail to comprehend that there can even be a peculiar harmony between good and evil. "Von Zeit zu Zeit seh' ich den Alten gern," says Mephistopheles. (From time to time I'm glad to see the Old One.)[5]

Harmony is difficult to perceive when we adopt an exclusively vertical or exclusively horizontal scale of values. When all is said and done, harmony cannot be perceived only from without. One must be in the midst of it, as well. Harmony can enable us to understand what we have said above, namely, that victory, even that of "the good guys," never leads to peace.

"Harmony" means not only a *coincidentia oppositorum* but also a space in which there is room for all, without unitary reductionisms.

One of the most paradoxical and extraordinary sentences in literature is represented by Dante's effort to explain this fundamental harmony. Hell is the work of wisdom and love. Over the gates of hell, an inscription proclaims that this place has been created by the Holy Trinity: "La divina Potestate, somma Sapienza, e'l primo Amore."[6] If this harmony disappears from our consciousness, then the traditional hell loses its raison d'être. It does not exist. It is an aberration. Catherine of Genoa went even further. To the question whether anything could exist that would be worse than hell, she replied: "Yes, if it did not exist." Without it, no just harmony would be possible, in the medieval worldview.

This may be the most profound paradoxical expression of the meaning of harmony. Without harmony (and we can say, without inner, outer, political, and so on, harmony) it is impossible to speak of the experience and reality of peace. Peace is harmony. Not even hell destroys it. Hell is the dialectical possibility of harmony in the comprehensive conception of reality as maintained by many traditional religions.

We cite these examples in order to show that neither is harmony a bucolic idyll, nor peace a honeymoon. It is another matter whether the worldview today ought to be the same as that of our medieval predecessors.

Much has been written about harmony, from the time of Pythagoras and the Orphic rites down to our own days, with Leibniz, of course, holding an especially prominent place in the line.[7] The central idea expresses concatenation and order. Concatenation underscores the objective aspect. There must be an interrelationship among the parts of a whole in order that there be harmony. Order emphasizes the subjective aspect. Someone must discover the concatenation and see it as an order. But we are saying more than this. We are saying, first, that harmony implies totality, something comprehensive. Harmony embraces subject and object, knower and known. And second, we are saying that, by its very nature, harmony belongs to the ultimate structure of the universe.[8] If all of the processes of the universe were to function in some other way, that way would be the ultimate model, and on that basis we would be able to pass judgment on everything that is. That would be the harmonious way. That the universe is harmonious is a qualified tautology. What ought to be cannot ultimately depend on more than what it is.

For us, this means that harmony, a dimension of peace, cannot be an ideal conception of "ours," a projection of "ours" of what harmony ought to be. In other words, peace cannot be imposed from without. Peace must not be identified with *our* concept of peace. Peace must be founded on the very nature of things, founded in the real harmony of the universe. For example, if it is true that the material universe subsists thanks to the fact that the big fish eats the little fish, then harmony and peace cannot consist in managing to keep people from hunting, although it will demand that they hunt according to the natural rhythm of things (in order to subsist, not to accumulate; in order to share in the universal symbiosis, not to make money; and so on). In a word, peace cannot be antinatural or violent, although, of course, these notions are open to various interpretations.

Pythagoras, according to Porphyry, taught: "In nature a thing has a beginning, a middle, and an end. On the basis of this form and this nature, the number three has been proclaimed."[9]

Without entering into Pythagorean numerology, let us recall that three is traditionally the perfect number. It expresses the harmony of everything that exists.[10] Peace, as well, has a triadic structure. It is more than a dual tension or a monarchical dominion. It implies a relation, so to speak, which is never closed up in a monistic short circuit or exhausted in a dualistic struggle. Peace seems to require a constant flux from one thing to another, without ever a return by the same route—an ongoing giving and receiving. This is what we mean to suggest when we indicate that the basis of peace is harmony. "All problems of existence are essentially problems of harmony," wrote Sri Aurobindo in the exordium of his *chef d'oeuvre*.[11]

Freedom

In the segment on the left of the peace sign is *freedom*. And here, "left" has a certain "political" connotation. A certain ideology of the "left" seems more sensitive to freedom than to order.

What is certain is that freedom is an essential ingredient of peace. Without freedom, there is no peace. And to say "freedom" is tantamount to saying: freedom of the individual, political freedom, group freedom, freedom of the earth, freedom of matter, freedom of animals, freedom of microbes, and so on. To invoke an example: Ayurvedic medicine does not kill microbes (which then return in force), but localizes them, so that, once they are corralled, so to speak, they will no longer proliferate. It is not correct to say, as one often hears, that the proliferation of bacteria is bad for people but good for the bacteria. We cannot overcome anthropocentric thinking unless we eliminate anthropomorphism. It would be an evil for us—who are not bacteria—if bacteria were to restrict our freedom. But it is not an evil for the bacteria that their antihomeostatic growth should cease to be stimulated. The proliferation of the bacteria also represents an evil for them, and for the universe as a whole. Liberty is not license.

"Freedom" does not mean mere "freedom of choice." A wider range of choices is sometimes consonant with a diminished freedom. To be able to choose this or that in a supermarket, or to be able to vote for this candidate or that, along a limited spectrum of possibilities, means a very relative freedom, and sometimes merely an apparent one: the options are restricted to what the supply offers. Man's freedom is antecedent to, and deeper than, the ability to choose. "Freedom" means absence of determination from without, from dependency, from alien influences, in such a way that my being can manifest itself, develop, according to what it is, without coercion from without or indoctrination from within. Freedom consists in doing, thinking, acting, and so on, in conformity with what one is.

If much has been written about harmony, discussions on freedom are endless.[12] For the case before us, we shall limit ourselves to saying that "freedom" implies self-determination, although very different ideas may be held regarding the nature of this *self* that "determines itself," and there can be many interpretations of the meaning of "determination."[13] We also prescind from any treatment of the manipulations of freedom, so familiar in democratic technocracies, calculated to please voters and win their votes. Nor shall we enter upon sociological considerations.[14] Our commentary will be restricted to the thesis that an imposed peace is a contradiction: that there is no peace without freedom, and that authentic peace can be won only in a regime of freedom. For our purposes, we can equivalate freedom with an acknowledgment of the dignity of the person, which, accordingly, is incompatible with the degradation of that person to a mere means or a simple tool for "higher" ends. Depriving people of their freedom, which the prevailing penitentiary system seems to think is the right way to go about things, must be included on any list of threats to peace. The criminal underworld, so frequently made up of ex-cons, knows all about that. What we have nowadays is a secularized christian *theologoumenon*. In bygone times, penances were imposed in an effort to convert the sinner, and it was believed that a certain reparation won forgiveness for the fault. To this end, punishment was applied. No state believes in this today.

Today, simply, those who have transgressed the law are deprived of freedom, and are sometimes sentenced to prison terms of hundreds of years, as with the old "indulgences"! Here we have another case of mental inertia. The only thing we assert is that the "penitentiary" system (as it is still called) is not an institution of peace.

Our first ingredient for peace—harmony—helps us to resolve the so-called "conflict of freedoms," a concept that so often has served to crush quantitative or qualitative minorities. Obviously there are conflicts among the aspirations of different individuals. All freedom presupposes self-determination within an accepted, acknowledged, or simply given order. Not everything is as simple as traffic regulations. Men are not machines running on wheels, constrained to travel preconstructed routes. Neither a car nor its driver is a free being. Personal freedom means the recognition, one's own as well as others', of a person's *ontonomy*. The premise of ontonomy is that the ultimate structure of reality is harmonious, and that consequently the plenitude of one being stands in a relation with the perfection of the totality.

But there is more. Freedom is an antimechanistic notion. Without now entering upon considerations of scientific apologetics, modern physics itself teaches us that even the laws of nature are indeterministic. The order or harmony of freedom is not automatically predictable, is not subject to once-for-all legislation, does not suppose a ready-made, determined universe. Human freedoms are not statistically expressible factors, unlike those called—with meaningful irony—"degrees of freedom" in statistics.

This means that peace cannot be based on an immutable order, in a fixed, predetermined structure. Peace is not something like a field in which, after the calculation of each individual's respective degree of freedom, behavior is legislated that will respect those degrees. In other words: peace cannot be legislated once and for all— it would not be peace—any more than love can be commanded—it would not be love. Peace has nothing in common with the rigidity of a freedom in which each atom is assigned a determined space lest it disturb its neighbor. Peace must be created and re-created, continuously. Its analogue here is the *creatio continua* of christian scholasticism, which, being a free act of the Creator, has incorporated the latter's freedom into the very nature of things.

If peace implies and requires a regime of freedom, and if freedom means respect for the ontonomy of the human person, it follows immediately that peace cannot be imposed. It must be received, earned, created, as we have been saying. There is no peace in the presence of a tyranny or dictatorship of any kind, individual or institutional, sacred or profane.

To put it another way: the ultimate subject of freedom is not the individual, but being, reality in its totality. If individuals seek to isolate themselves from the totality, they will never be free. They will be tyrants if they are more powerful than their neighbors, but the latter will continue to impose conditions on them, if only negatively. Another person, in his or her quality as *aliud,* some*thing* else, will always be alienating, hence coercive. Only when the *aliud* is discovered to be *alius/a,* some*one* else—another "I"—can he or she be converted into a *you* and come to form part of our supraindividual identity, so that her or his challenges will be no longer just a series of coercions of our freedom, but a higher form of freedom. Without love, then, there is no freedom, as the wisdom of the ages knows so well. Freedom, before being a right of the individual, is a character of reality. Hence, it is not a question of my *ego* renouncing its freedom in order that other *ego*s may also be free, but rather a matter of factoring their freedom by diluting myself as an individual and appearing as a person. Only one resurrected is free—and a factor for peace, then.

A culture of peace must be a culture of freedom. Now, in the scientific and technological world in which we live, a world governed by quantitative laws right down to the voting laws, the profound freedom of the individual sees itself constantly restricted. It will be said that taboos, and the weight of tradition, also restricted the freedom of individuals. I answer that, in the first place, the sanction of tradition was believed to be of a superior order, and one's submission to it was not interpreted as a forced submission to the will of the majority on the part of those who did not belong to that majority. But in the second place—and this is the important thing—we must say that what we are advocating is not a return to old schemas. My metaphysical thesis, which it would be beside the point to explicitate here, is that the Parmenidean binary of being and thinking leaves no room for freedom of being: being is constrained to obey thinking.[15] The culture of freedom demands other premises.

Justice

The area on the right in the peace sign represents *justice.* And indeed right-wing ideologies seem to have more affinity for a just order than for a presumably more dangerous freedom. But here too we have to say that justice is an essential ingredient of peace. Without justice there is no peace. And "justice" denotes not only the Roman concept of *iustitia*, it includes that of the *dharma* as well, among many other things.

The *dharma*, as its very root indicates (*dhr:* take, store, sustain), is the element of cohesiveness in the universe, the celebrated *lokasamgraha* of the Gītā.[16] It is the *dharma*, indeed, that maintains peoples.[17] The *dharma* is justice—the fitting order and natural place of things. Thus, justice stands in direct contradiction with violence. Its relation to peace is traditional, and it is the obligatory theme of a philsophy of peace. *"Opus iustitiae pax"* (the work and deed of justice is peace).[18]

Iustitia et pax osculatae sunt, prays one of the psalms.[19] Justice, peace, and joy are characteristics of the reign of God,[20] says Paul, in a passage that has not been the object of adequate meditation. The criterion is gladness (*chara*)—joy in the Spirit.

An unjust peace is not only fragile and fleeting. It is not peace at all, properly speaking. For our purposes, let us limit ourselves to saying that justice attributes to each being that which belongs to it— what is that being's own, and its due: *suum cuique,* "to each his/her/its own."[21] Here too the trait emerges that we have seen in the other two ingredients of peace. Justice is a fundamental relation. Justice refers to our relations with others. Analogously, peace is not an interioristic affair, having only an inner dimension. Inward peace requires and demands outward peace, as we have said.

The major problem of peace in its relation with justice consists in its cultivation and acquisition in situations of injustice, especially institutionalized injustice.

The recent case of the Gulf War offers an extreme example, but the same can be said of the situation in Latin America, and so many other cases, such as the Italian Mafia, or work or family situations in which injustice reigns—at times, chronic, age-old injustice. The example of the inveterate injustices of patriarchal societies toward women is another example of major proportions.

The first example cited just above, by reason of its very bellicosity and extremism, is paradigmatic. We are shocked at an isolated case of injustice: the invasion of Kuwait by Iraq. But this act is isolated in our minds as well, and we are insensitive to the accumulation of injustices in that region of the world over the course of centuries, especially, since World War I. Now, if, in order to justify the existence of the state of Israel, we appeal to the fact that the Hebrew people once occupied the Land of Promise, then why not go back just before that and say that Palestine really belongs to the Canaanites, from whom the Hebrews wrested it so violently and treacherously? There is a principle of jurisprudence called "prescription," according to which a person's right to something expires after a certain length of time during which that right has not been exercised. Then is Israel's current policy justified—that of "waiting" for time to heal the injustice—as the lesser evil? What if that turns out to be a strategem?[22] Shall we then have to go back to Adam and Eve? Shall we attempt to justify a struggle against a state on grounds that that state was founded on an injustice that yet perdures? Will peace then be the resignation of the vanquished, or some utopian dream?

Three considerations are in order. *First:* Peace is a problem precisely because it presents itself as a goal in an unpeaceful situation. Just as the true problem of tolerance arises in the presence of concrete intolerance, so the authentic problem of peace arises when one finds oneself in confrontation with unjust situations. It is easy enough to orate about justice as a cause and condition of peace. But that does not solve the problem. To think that, in order to attain peace, or live at peace, we must go back to the beginning, to the *status ante pacem,* is tantamount to declaring peace to be impossible. We shall simply be grabbing at the facile gimmick of a *natura corrupta,* which thereupon justifies all injustice, violence, and war. Have we not yet avenged Abel? We have criticized interiorism—the withdrawal of peace to the sphere of the individual and interior. Peace is relational, and every relation has at least two poles.

Two considerations impel us not to accept simple interior peace as a sufficient answer. One is precisely that peace is inseparable from justice. And justice, as we have said, is a relation. And relation is constitutive of the human person and all reality. One cannot have peace, not even interior peace, if one isolates oneself from the world. The attitude of the bodhisattva or the christian is the most realistic. We are all set in a relation, and are interdependent. *Pratītyasamutpāda* and *nirvāṇa,* original sin and the mystic body of Christ, are a reality. The true solitude of the mystic is not selfish isolation. The authentic monk enters into solitude in order to defeat and transcend isolation.[23]

Another consideration militating against the interiorism of seeking a merely inner peace by detaching oneself from the madding crowd is in the inherent elitism (if not selfishness) of such a posture. Very few of us can withdraw from involvement in outward injustices, not for want of any moral courage, but by reason of human impossibility. To think that one can withdraw to a *merely* inner peace if one has sufficient spiritual formation, intellectual cognition, and

71

socioeconomic comfort, is to forget that Man is a person and not just an individual. Circumstances affect human beings, too. My "I" includes my "circumstance" (Ortega y Gasset), and the latter, in many cases, does not allow me such and such a comfortable distance. If the snipers are in the street, if exploitation is rampant, if it is a matter of my children's bread or my own subsistence, if withdrawal from the *res publica* is not neutrality but cowardice, if not wanting to make a difficult decision is thereby to make a cowardly decision, if I live in more or less of a concentration camp, if . . . and so on, then it is impossible to speak of an exclusively interior peace, because my very interior has been invaded by exteriority.

Let us repeat: If anyone *thinks* that suffering is always ennobling, that oppression does not necessarily demean a person to the level of an animal, or that misery is not degrading, this is because that person is *thinking* about all of this, and has not been deprived of his or her very thinking. It is all the more urgent to be the voice of the voiceless when the voiceless have become not only aphonic, but mute: they no longer have anything to say. We cannot make a meditation on peace while comfortably entrenched in our manifold fortresses.[24]

The *second* consideration to which we have referred is the following. Justice must not be confused with legality.[25] Peace is not content with lawfulness. Peace aspires to justice. But justice does not materialize in a vacuum. Here we collide with the excruciating problem of means and ends. Most wars have been undertaken on the pretext of defending justice. A "just cause"—it has been said since Saint Augustine—is the first requisite for the justification of an act of war. We shall not enter on this consideration, but only observe that, if one extreme consists in the purism of a concern for the reestablishment of an order that has been disturbed—disturbed perhaps since the very origin of Man—and another extreme is rebellion against any unjust order, a third extreme will consist in a more or less fatalistic resignation, and a tumble into the trap of mere lawfulness. Here we are criticizing not only certain religious doctrines that inculcate a fatalistic resignation or eschatological patience, but also a certain absolutization of democracy, which tolerates only the opposition that respects the intangible game rules and "sacrosanct" values of national "constitutions" that are usually opposed by those who have not voted for them. Need we recall the slaves in the time of Pericles, or the three-quarters of the French, after the Revolution of 1789, who were not allowed to vote because they were unable to pay the poll tax? Or need we remind ourselves of the Constitution of the United

States itself, which excluded slaves and blacks? Peace is not synonymous with "lawfulness," because lawfulness is not justice. Many dictatorships are perfectly legal. The realization of peace, then, calls for more than sophists, attorneys, and politicians. The realization of peace calls for more than attachment to an antecedently established legality. Peace and justice alike demand more. And this brings us to our next comment.

The *third* consideration is that peace, like justice, points to transcendence, to something accepted as indisputable and regarded as outside the interplay of factors that help or hinder peace. We understand "transcendence" here in its literal sense: something out beyond the ingredients of a question. The model example, possibly, is God. But it could likewise be any other prevailing myth. Above, we have cited the Constitution, and democracy, and we have indicated the state. A recognition that the establishment of peace requires a criterion, a norm or pole that enables us to speak of peace and that transcends the litigating parties, is no problem whatsoever. The phenomenology of transcendency is not very problematic. The difficult thing is its material recognition, its concrete notion. Hence our discussion on myth. Myth is indisputable, simply because it is not disputed. An example will spare us some ink. One may think that today's military system is unjust, and accordingly, that not only military laws but all laws that constrain citizens to accept obligatory military service and military authority are unjust.[26] One may even think that the institution of the armed forces is the greatest obstacle to peace. It is obvious that legality is not on this person's side. Many others will attack such an opinion, reproaching it with being not only naive, but unjust to society, which in such a hypothesis would be rendered "defenseless." Our intention here is not to broach a discussion of this specific matter, but to examine its very foundation. Our example is not that of the conscientious objector, which is confined to the decision of the individual and to the series of risks that such a decision might entail. Our example is a problem not of individualistic morality, but one that concerns a society's justice, without which a real, lasting peace cannot be established. The sole plausible justification is for one to embrace with all one's heart—in all sincerity—something like, "God wills it," or "Uncle Sam wants you," or "Society has thus disposed," or "The law is the law," and so on. That is, the only plausible justification is that one recognize a transcendency on which one confers an authority that conjures away all scruples of conscience.

This problem cannot be sidestepped in any serious reflection on peace. The most flagrant case is that of the guerrilla war and what is called "terrorism." If violence is not the solution, still less will state or legal violence be. As long as the two parties do not commune in the same myth, there will be no peace. But myth is the acknowledgment of the transcendent. In order that there be peace on earth, the angels of heaven must sing (Luke 2:14). In translation, that means that, without a radical anthropological and cosmological change, individuals cannot democratically bestow upon themselves the peace that they so rationally desire. The parameters are different.

As we have seen, a mere description of what peace is stirs the most profound questions concerning the nature of the human being and of reality.

COMPLEXITY OF PEACE

We have described the three ingredients of peace, and the problems have mounted. We have yet to examine the proportion of these ingredients. How to combine harmony, freedom, and justice? Which of them is to rule the others? When we attempt to impose— in the name of God, or a certain concept of justice, or a party, a race, a civilization, a culture, or a religion—a certain order, peace does not follow. Our triadic symbol implies a confidence precisely in the trinity that constitutes it. A fundamental human act consists in one's self-recognition as living reality. This acknowledgment leads to a kind of *cosmic confidence,* in which reality is real.[27] Where, beyond the real, could we place our trust? We have neither the duty nor the power either to create or to justify reality. We have to live reality, and by living it, transform it. Reality is not simply there. It becomes, of course, and we cooperate in the endeavor. But this very activity belongs to reality. That means that experience enjoys a primacy over experiment, consciousness of life over thinking. Experience, as its very name suggests, is a traversing of something immediately given. Experiment manipulates the data, but ultimately must have recourse to experiences that are irreducible to others. In the case before us, none of our three elements (harmony, freedom, and justice) has the hegemony over the others. None is manipulable at the expense of the others. Circularity and interdependence are constitutive. Herein consists concord, as the last strophe of the Vedas sings, as does the western tradition that goes back to Heraclitus and is summarized in the consecrated expression, *concordia discors.*[28]

What we wish to indicate with all of this consists of two thoughts. The first is that cosmic confidence in necessity is the ontological premise for even knowing what mistrust is. We shall not now enter into the theological problem of monotheism or the philosophical problem of being. We shall limit ourselves to a description of this sort of cosmic trust in a reality that is simply given, that is here, that we have not ourselves made. Reality is *causa sui,* said the old philosophers. Reality has no need of anyone to "check up on it" in order to be, or of any argument in order to be proved. On what would such a check, or argument, be based? Unless one existed, one could not inquire into one's existence. The question of being or nothingness would not be posed, were there no one existing to pose it. The degree of objectivity of our experience is another matter. Our only point: cosmic confidence—which differs from epistemological certitude as well as from the concrete interpretation we give this trust—is an ontic necessity superior to the logical principle of non-contradiction. Peace is based on it.

The second thought to which we have referred expresses the dynamism of all reality, which moved Pythagorean Philolaos of Croton to say: "Harmony consists in the union of multiple things mixed, and in the community of spirit of those who think in divergent ways."[29] Peace is not a static reality.

This leads us to a new consideration with regard to the peace sign. The three fields of peace are delimited by a circle. This symbolizes three more aspects of peace—a *circle* of *equal, centered* spaces.

The *circle* represents the fact that peace is limited by its surface, and unlimited by its circumference. Peace is not infinite, as neither is a circle. It is no different with our concrete human condition and particular situation. There is no such thing as an infinite peace. Peace is a tangible, concrete, limited thing, which it is possible to enjoy. It is not a utopia. Peace is on a human scale, although it can always grow— just as a circle, too, can become larger. But peace can grow only on one condition. Peace can grow only on condition that the circle "hold"—that is, that it keep equidistant from the center, that it keep a balance among its three fields, so that the latter remain equal.

Now, a circle is limited by its own circumference, and the latter is indefinite in itself. A circumference has no beginning or end: any point can be its beginning, and at any point we can postulate that it ends. But what constitutes the circumference is its center. The circumference refers to, bears on, its center and nothing else. Now, as every point is equidistant from the center, we have no natural criterion for saying where the circumference begins and where it ends. Peace, like human plenitude, is undefined. Every person, and each society, has his, her, and its own peace or its own lack of peace.

The fact that the three spaces must be *equal* signifies the balance that ought to reign among harmony, freedom, and justice in order that there be peace. Any imbalance alters this. The balance is precisely peace, but it cannot be established by any of its parts. If this balance, this peace, "commands" justice, as it were, freedom and harmony will suffer. And the same can be said of the dominion of either of the other two. Hence the fact that many traditions have declared peace to be a gift: something given—and received—but incapable of being manipulated, even by the will, however "good" the latter might be.

Finally—as we have said—in order that the three spaces may be equal within the circle, they need to be *centered* on the same center of the circumference that shapes the cross of peace. This center is the locus of love. Love centers the three ingredients of peace and is the criterion of their equilibrium. There is no question, obviously, of a love that is pure sentiment or pure will. Rather, the love of which we are speaking here is the love the ancients called *eros,* the gospel *agapē,* and the Vedas *kāma,* which "was in the beginning,"[30] and which, being the "first germ" of life, is "more sublime than the gods."[31] We are referring, obviously, to that primordial force that is the "naturalis motus omnium rerum,"[32] which moves the whole *hōs erōmenon,* "as something loving,"[33] and of which Dante wrote, so compendiously, "l'amor che muove il sole e l'altre stelle" (the love that moves the sun and the other stars).[34] Human peace, then, the peace of our experience, is not the ultimate reality. Peace seems to have an intriguing instability.

We wish to indicate that, in its complexity, peace is neither natural nor supernatural. It is *not natural* because, in the ensemble of the elements that make up peace, each of them seems to tend to invade the terrain of the others, that is, to destroy what medicine calls "homeostasis." Countries overly concerned with justice restrict freedom. And vice versa: where freedom is sacrosanct, justice frequently suffers. And with too much harmony, "your neighbors invade you."

Peace is *not supernatural,* because if it were, we should have to begin all over again. Who possesses pure revelation, uncontaminated by contingent human interpretations, so as to be able to dictate the adequate relation that ought to prevail among the three sectors in question? To confuse religion with ethics is to run a great risk. A supreme ethical principle, a criterion of good and evil, would in some sense be superior to good and evil itself, which is a contradiction even for ethics.

Perhaps we ought to say (although this, too, will be an imperfect formula) that peace is *metanatural.*

To sum up—after this series of considerations which, perforce, has contained a great deal of analysis—I should define peace, following the nondualistic view that has inspired us from the outset, in the following manner:

Peace is not a simple state of mind, but is rather a state of be-ing (the gerund), a state of Being (as a noun denoting all reality). Peace is that state of Being corresponding to the being in question. That is, peace is a welfare in Being. When a being is in its place, it is at peace. When a bone, an individual, or a society is not in its place, it is not at peace. The bone hurts, the individual is disturbed, the society is unstable. And so with every being. But the spatial metaphor must be understood dynamically and freely. The "place" of which we speak is not a predetermined space, or static locality, in which each being occupies its spot in a rank and file as in a regiment on parade, nor is each part localized after the manner of a part functioning in a machine. Instead of "place," we could have said "duty." Peace emerges when a being complies with its duty. But here again the metaphor could be misunderstood. The duty in question is not an extrinsic one. Each being's ought-to-be is its being-where-it-belongs. "When each being fulfills its 'function' " might be a third formulation of the same notion.

That shows us that the difficulty will lie in the discovery of this "place," "duty," or "function." We have spoken above of the "cosmic order." A theist could call it the "will of God." A "state of be-ing," we said at the beginning—that state that corresponds to a be-ing. The difficulty abides. What criteria do we have to discern that "state" or that "will"? None, except tautological ones! One is in one's place when one has peace, and one has peace when one is in one's place. There is peace when a society is integrated into the cosmic order, and when a society is integrated into the cosmic order there is peace. The "will of God" gives me peace when I know that it is God's will, and I know that it is God's will when I have peace! Precisely because peace pertains to the ultimate order of things, the situation could be no other. There is no ulterior reference point. It will be said that an out-of-place tibia hurts, because its place is visible to everyone; while the place of an individual—as this depends, among other things, on that individual's own will—cannot be known with such precision, since this same will, being free, will frequently have doubts about its decisions. A community has peace when it is integrated into an internal and external order that permits the ontonomic realization of all of its components. But peace is the very criterion.

Matters become even more complicated when we incorporate

the mystery of evil into our argument. Peace is a relation. I—as an individual or as a society—can be very much at peace with myself and with others; but suddenly a greedy enemy rises up, seeking to rob me or invade me. My peace has been disturbed by an extrinsic factor. Now I must make a decision that is all the more difficult for the fact that I know that I have given some occasion for this violation of my peace by these outsiders.

However, all of this only carries us to a far deeper and more realistic conception of peace. It shows us, in the first place, that peace is not a static state, and that, accordingly, it is found to be constantly *in fieri*. In the second place, it shows us that peace is neither purely subjective nor exclusively objective. It is relational. In the third place, it shows us that peace is never perfect—that is, that it is never finished and complete. In the fourth place, it shows us that peace is not available to precise definitions, because of its character of ultimacy. In the fifth place, it shows us that peace has no biunivocal relation with the rest of reality. I can be at peace with others without others being at peace with me. In the sixth place, it shows us that peace is not a monolithic block. It is polyfaceted, and even pluralistic. It has facets, degrees, nuances. It is not subject to quantification, since these very facets are not homogeneous. And finally, it shows us that peace is the relation that joins us, equitably and with freedom, to a harmonious whole.

8 Obstacles to Peace

If, at first sight, peace looks to be impossible of realization, it also presents itself as something to be realized: after all, it is never fully realized. The realization of peace collides with countless obstacles, many of which are obvious, although that does not make them less important. The ambition to have "more at any cost," on the part of individuals or entire countries, is an example.[1] A whole series of ethical problems is in the foreground here: problems of justice (the just distribution of wealth), of the freedom of the person, and so many others. Anything that, in one way or another, wounds any of the three ingredients of peace, represents an obstacle to peace.

By no means must we omit the moral questions. If men were "good," if they did not exploit their fellows, if they used technology with moderation, if they effected a better distribution of what they have received, and eliminated resentment, greed, and hatred, then obviously a great deal would have been gained in the direction of the establishment of peace among human beings. The existential problem lies in the conditional "if" that governs the whole sentence. A certain pragmatic moral theory has argued whether it would not actually be more advantageous to one's own self-interest to be moral and always to tell the truth. And yet, the "if" remains as problematic as it is disobeyed. *"Ethos anthrōpō daimōn,"* Heraclitus said (Man's behavior stems from his spirit).[2]

But we shall keep faithful to the title of our study, and refrain from heading down these roads, which are being amply dealt with by a growing number of authorities. Rather we shall concentrate on structural problems of the modern culture that we are attempting to disarm. Without this disarmament, we insist, no effort for peace will be lasting. Not that we mean to ignore or slight the ethical problems. On the contrary, the ethical is at the base, and supplies us with the energy we shall need in order to overcome the institutional obstacles that we are about to mention. Without the ethical thrust that conquers ambition, selfishness, and unlove, our analysis would be inoperative. On the supposition, then, of the morality of the person, we shall restrict ourselves to a consideration of three major obstacles.

THE MILITARY

Our first obstacle might be dubbed the "degeneration of the military." There has been a gradual evolution in our awareness and justification of the military estate, culminating in the current mutation. I shall begin with some praise for the military. And it goes without saying that I have no intention of calling in question the goodwill and—the word was never more suitably used—the "chivalry," the gallantry, of today's military. Here would be an application of what I have said, on many occasions, about mental inertia.

From the viewpoint of the history of religions, the military, the *ksatriyas*, the nobility, the warriors, are one of culture's most extraordinary creations. It is the soldier, in the classic sense, who has the function of *lokasamgraha,* as the Bhagavad Gītā would say—the maintenance of the cosmic cohesion of the universe. The nobility, the military, have a stricter code than have others, since their duty is to offer the cosmic sacrifice that maintains the world and the universe in cohesion. The brahmins are at the orders of the *ksatriyas.* The military represents defense in the face of the assaults of the invader, and the warranty of security. The social order is based on the same tripartite schema of functions that the cosmic order is. It comprises representatives of Heaven (the priesthood in its manifold acceptations), Earth (business people and laborers), and Man (the soldier and the politician). I am being very summary. The reader need only consult G. Dumézil (without necessarily accepting all his theses) in order to understand what is being suggested here.[3] It is the knight who has the task of supporting the widow, the pauper, the invalid, the pilgrim, and so on. Consider the military orders. Military personnel are perhaps the only ones today to hold on to the old-fashioned uniform, along with their music, their braids and chevrons, and their swords. The soldier is not permitted things that others may be. The ritual sense of life is still preserved in the military spirit. The life of the soldier is a model of virtues. The very word "virtue" is instructive: its etymology refers to the positive qualities typifying the *vir*, the male human being, who is basically the knight—that is, the warrior. Homer's *aretē* is precisely military, and only later—with Aristotle, especially—does it come to be regarded as a civilian quality.

This state of affairs has been undergoing an evolution, with a consequent degeneration and culminating in a mutation. The reason for its degeneration is power. The reason for its mutation is technocratic modernity. And so the military institution today is a caricature of what it once was.[4] We ought to stop producing war literature, Virgil warns—"Ne tanta animis adsuescite bella."[5]

Let us have a theological digression. When the Second Vatican Council sought to condemn atomic weapons, at the instigation of one of its five Moderators—Cardinal Lercaro—the theologians did not realize, so far as I know, that the Second Lateran Council (1139), in its Canon 29, had already condemned nuclear missiles and bombs *ante litteram,* and this under pain of excommunication.[6] Arms are licit only if and when they constitute an extension of the human arm, as is the case with the spear and the sword. The utilization of these latter arms, called "white" arms, calls for the activity of the entire being of the warring subject. It is not my brute strength that does battle, but my whole being, for I am an instrument of the divine justice. Thus, if I have not the necessary concentration, which requires serenity and peace of soul, then reason is not with me. We need only think of those judgments of God, the jousts, and the whole Japanese theory of the martial arts. Obviously, without God's help I shall be wounded or vanquished, since I shall not have all that I require in order to be the victor: after all, it is not physical strength that counts, but the whole ensemble of reality. The struggle is still something in which the very Gods are engaged. But we could assign a less providentialistic and more psychological explanation: the whole force of the spirit is concentrated in the arm when that spirit is pure, and gathers all the available energy of the universe. The moment weapons are disjoined from the arm and "deadly" weapons, long-distance weapons, are invented, their power becomes independent of Man, and is converted into brute force—into a simple destructive power. The stronger, not the more just, wins. The more astute wins, not the nobler. And this is in itself intrinsically evil. The weapon is no longer an extension of Man, but an independent force. With nuclear weapons, obviously, things have completely changed. The evolution is complete, and degenerate.[7]

81

It is false that war is a natural phenomenon. There is a quite convincing literature on this today. The works of Fromm, of Konrad Lorenz, of Eibl-Eibesfeldt, and so many others, show that animals do not wage war. War is a ritual act, and successively, the degeneration of that rite. No natural aggressivity of ours leads to war.[8] Peace is a *metanatural phenomenon,* as we said. War is a *cultural phenomenon.* As civilization grows, war, in a certain sense, waxes apace. As Lewis Mumford said, the essence of civilization is the exercise of power. Without any attempt just now to tally up the frequency of wars, the European case is instructive. Every century since 1500 has seen more wars than the previous century. In the sixteenth century, Europeans fought 87 battles; in the seventeenth, 239; in the eighteenth, 781; in the nineteenth, 651; and in the first forty years of the twentieth century, 892 battles were fought, according to statistics compiled by Wright and cited by Erich Fromm.[9] The number of the wounded and killed in the first wars was 0.01 percent of the total population. Now it is 13 percent. We now have thirty million persons permanently under arms, and we have already listed some of the data. Have we need of much further discussion on the degeneration of war, the mutation of its meaning, its antinaturality, and the problematic status of the armed forces?

All of this is all the more significant for the fact that the *ius ad bellum,* which before World War I was still regarded as a right vested in every sovereign state, has been proscribed in a goodly proportion of modern constitutions.

After the mercenary armies, which were in the majority until the eighteenth century, came "obligatory military service." This was seen as a sign of progress. It proclaimed that the defense of the nation was incumbent upon every citizen capable of assisting therein. But the noble motive of defending one's homeland was transformed into a naive idealism when the "art of war" attained a higher ratio of technification. Once more, mercenaries were needed, now called "military advisers."

Montesquieu had felt it coming.[10] The moment science was placed at the service of the armed forces, the duty of defense was transformed into competition for destructive capacity.

All of this leads us to a consideration of the advisability not only of unilateral disarmament, but also the abolition of the military institution, utopian as that may appear to those who call themselves "realists" and who make their option for a "lesser evil." The question is whether their option is not perhaps for the greater evil, and whether the real problem is to be able to discern a third alternative—

besides, obviously, determining the intermediate steps to the goal of the said emancipation of the military. Ordinary folk are beginning to wonder whether the greatest obstacle to peace will not be precisely the very existence of military institutions. But we are under no obligation to get down to practical details in this study, despite our acknowledgment of their importance.

TECHNOCRATIC CIVILIZATION

A second characteristic of modern culture as an obstacle to peace is technocracy. We have already spoken of this, but we shall add three more considerations: the human scale; the nature of technocracy; modern science.

The Human Scale

Technocracy, besides destroying the human scale, represents the abandonment of the measure proper to Man and its replacement with the measure proper to the machine. This may well be another "transfer" of the divine infinitude to a spatial and human "unlimitedness."[11] But at all events, at least in the case of the ecosystem, it destroys the equilibrium that is an indispensable condition for peace. The technocratic Man is no longer a biped, but a "rotable"—a being on wheels; no longer a knight, but a coach driver; no longer *homo loquens* but *homo pulsans atque telematicus* (button-pressing and remote-controlling). No longer speaks, but amplifies his or her decibels, and passes on information that is no longer communication. Neither walks nor mounts, but rolls or flies. And all this on a grand scale, a broadened scale. The person is a simple factor that must shift over great distances, and make his or her contribution to be processed, thereby to become a simple factor in a grand network of information. Imagine a "citizen" without wheels, telephone, newspapers, or a job involving thousands of coproducers and consumers. He will not survive—he will be displaced. The *inter*dependence of autochthonous beings has been transformed into an *intra*dependency of functional, and furthermore, easily replaceable, parts. No one believes himself or herself unique, since no one believes himself or herself some*one*. The individual is a minimal cog in the gears of the megamachine. Standing before the Pyramid of Cheops, a Man is small, and may feel afraid unless he belongs to the clan; standing before the Pentagon in Washington, he is outright insignificant, and may well feel terror unless he is part of the system.

In technocratic civilization, everything is remote-controlled, not from above, but from afar (by computers, the law of supply and demand, needs and conveniences, and so on). Traditional interventions "from above" (providence, fate, *karma*, and the like), by virtue of an intrinsic demand of peace, had a transcendent origin. In technocratic civilization, immediacy, if not spontaneity, has been lost, since nearly everything is calculable, and, at least statistically, foreseeable. Fortunately—as this same adverb shows, recalling the Goddess Fortune—modern Man does not only live on technocracy (live from, and live under, the power of technology). But if a flight to the inner world, while difficult, is possible, escape from the outer world is practically impossible. We live and move and have our being in an artificial world. Peace, too, comes out prefabricated and fake.

Some will say that this is Man's future: everything is calculable, everything is foreseeable. Breathing will be artificial, just as food and the air. "Services" will function better, and Man will have been delivered from the slavery of work and the anguish of hunger and sickness. It is a consistent vision. Only the strongest and ablest will survive. This is the response we hear to the objection that a system that consumes more than one hundred times the available renewable energy will only permit the survival of one-fourth of our current population. Once more we have "natural selection," only that, this time, the "natural" selection is artificial.

The answer cannot be technological (a quest for better solutions), but must be anthropological (in terms of an answer to the question, What is Man?). But our problem is peace. And peace becomes impossible in this kind of perfected technocratic system, because it turns out to be superfluous: it is no longer a value. The craftiest, the ablest (not the most intelligent), or the strongest will impose *order*. What now is the natural order will be the order of those who take over the big technocratic machine. (I was about to write, "of those who will grasp the reins of the system," but techniculture has voided the agricultural metaphor.)

This poses humanity a fundamental option, which, for all its vagueness and difficulty, is nonetheless transcendental. Shall we have a technocratic regime on a planetary, indeed solar, scale, or shall we integrate ourselves once more into the rhythms of the earth and even the sun? Shall we choose acceleration or rhythm?

The option is vague, because the decision of an individual in a quantitative world is a "negligible quantity," as the thinkers of the eighteenth century said when they introduced the infinitesimal calculus. It is vague, furthermore, because it cannot be restricted to being merely negative, antitechnological, but must be a decision in favor of a viable order nowadays. And finally, it is vague because the

84

individual counts for so little, and individual effort is diluted in a collective mass that makes no decisions.

The decision is difficult, as well, becasue of the enormous power of technology. But to take no decision is itself to decide to bolster the strength of the majoritarian current. The solution is not easy, since a simple destruction of the technocratic apparatus is not feasible, nor would be conducive to peace. Elsewhere I have intimated some alternatives; but this is not what directly interests us now.

The Nature of Technocracy

The second consideration bears on the very nature of technocracy. I shall summarize it in nine propositions, more as points for discussion than as theses to be defended.[12]

1. There is an essential difference between technics or technique, in the sense of *technē*, and contemporary technocracy. A mutation, not a linear continuation (progress) of the traditional *technai* (arts), has taken place at the heart of a single culture. Technocracy is the dominant attribute of contemporary civilization.
2. Technocracy is more than applied science. It represents a cultural ensemble that might be called "technocratic civilization." The socioeconomic is as essential to it as is the scientific.
3. Technocracy is not neutral or universal, nor, therefore, is it open to universalization. It is not a cultural invariable. It is the fruit of a single culture, to which it is essentially tied.
4. Technocracy is autonomous, and therefore creates a "fourth world," a world that asserts its independence from Man, Nature, and the Gods.
5. Technocracy begins with a mechanistic and gravitational conception of the world and leads to the dominion of the machine. Its proper method is experimentation, not experience, and it only makes sense in a quantifiable universe.
6. Technocracy presupposes that Man is essentially different from nature, and its feudal liege. It presupposes that matter has no life.
7. Technocracy supposes that reality is objectifiable, and hence an object of thought.
8. Technocracy is founded on a nominalistic view of reality.
9. Technocracy believes that dominion and control of the "forces of nature" represents "progress" toward the perfection of Man and the universe.

These nine propositions, rather metaphorical in character,

85

could be complemented with a sociological reflection that would afford us an understanding of the bond prevailing between what we have just said and the significant fact that the four most important industries of the current culture are money, arms, advertising, and tourism.[13] We are also reminded that, currently (1992), the productive capacity of the industrial world exceeds by more than one-third the consumer capacity of the entire world. No wonder that the world foreign debt rises yearly, as do the number of the poor and the number of military conflicts.[14]

It might be said that technocracy is perhaps a unilateral, even "defective," civilization. But this would not prove that it is a major obstacle to peace. Before we determine that, we must still introduce our third consideration.

Modern Science

Our third consideration may be the most delicate. As it bears on a modern myth, it wounds our sensibilities. It is a matter of fairly general opinion that we need more command of ourselves and a better use of modern technology. Many would agree that we must not let ourselves come under the domination of the machine, and that we should progress in mind and spirit in order to keep pace with material development. But few will dare touch the taboo of modern science, which has made so many undeniable discoveries and has brought us so far in our knowledge of things. This is the myth. We have relativized everything else—from what the Aztecs thought to what Jesus Christ said—but not our science.

After a slow maturation of my reflection on the question, I have come to the conviction that one of the most profound causes of our state of things is modern science.[15] This proposition entails certain serious consequences, which I have attempted to study elsewhere.[16] I should like to express my conception in three points.

1. It is not unique.

In an attempt to synthesize the experience or wisdom that has become crystallized over the last six thousand years of human experience, the development of the last four hundred European years ought to be scaled down. I once heard the rector of an illustrious university say, at an international congress being held in his magnificent hall, that 40 percent of all the important scientists of the world were gathered there, and that 90 percent of those who have made humanity's great discoveries are alive in our day. Such blindness, ethnocentrism, and naiveté simply astounds me. It is suspect, to say the

86

least, to think that we are the only wise ones that there have ever
been in the world, and that those who came before us were no more
than forerunners of our Science.

Modern science is a stupendous creation of the human spirit.
It has achieved, in its field, conquests that no other civilization has
attained. But its field is not the whole field of knowledge, let alone
of the human. These are our other two points.

2. It is not knowledge.

Modern science is not science in the usual understanding of
this term. "Science" (*jñana, gnōsis, scientia*) means "knowledge."
And knowing is something like striking a vital communion with the
real, being together with that which is known. Cognition is a "cog-
nation," a being-born-together-with. Knowledge is union, compen-
etration, and so on: knowledge is an end in itself. Knowing entails
joy, because it is salvation: it saves Man from his limitation, and
opens out to the very confines of the universe. Knowing, in this full
sense, which is inseparable from loving, affords Man a living experience of what he is. Modern science is no longer knowledge in this
classical, traditional sense. Not all persons can be scientists. All, however, are called to be sages—wise tasters and samplers of reality.

It is very instructive to observe how the Oracle of Delphi has
been interpreted through the centuries. *Gnōthi seauton* (Know yourself) consists not in observing oneself as an object, but rather in coming to discover in oneself that one-self which is not the object of any
knowledge but precisely the subject of it.[17] The journey consists in
coming to *be* oneself: *isthi su* (be you); *tat tvam asi* (this is you);[18]
and so on. "Eternal life is this: to know you. . . ."[19] But this is not
the "knowledge" of modern science, despite the latter's appropria-
tion of the name.

From the outlook of peace, the argument runs as follows. If
science, *gnōsis*, is the most valuable thing there is, and if this science
is the privilege of a few, then a mortal inequality is struck in the heart
of Man, and we are opening the door to the most desperate competition. Precious little good it will do for scientists to declare that they
do not possess the universal panacea, and that they know perfectly
well the limits of scientific knowledge. The fact remains: science's
unshakable successes, and its symbiosis with modern technology,
have persuaded the people that "outside science is no salvation."
And indeed, unless you have a career in science, there is little to "eat"
today in the First World and its satellites. If the fundamental thing
for Man is knowing, and if this becomes (except for the elementary

necessities of life) the specialty of a few, then we are implanting in the human heart one of the causes of a lack of peace. A culture of peace cannot be an elitist culture with respect to what is fundamental for Man. All problems of education are included here. A culture of peace must dismantle contemporary systems of education. The problem is complex, however, and it is not our present task to give advice about it.

3. It is violent.

We shall limit ourselves to a mere sketch of the third point, which in a certain sense extends further than modern science. We are accustomed to use reason—unconsciously, in most instances—as a weapon. Our civilization is a civilization of armed reason. Our reason is no longer science, or wisdom, or experience. It is experiment and power. Our reason makes conquerors of us, it permits us to "con-vince" control, predict, grasp. Dialectic is an intellectual struggle, and very frequently, a war.[20]

If it is true that we use reason as a weapon, then what we have said about cultural disarmament as a condition for peace is understandable. First we must confront armed reason, and then defeat it. In Romance languages, for "I am right," one says, "I have reason": thus, I have con-vinced you, I have conquered you. But reason is not for having or for convincing. The intellect, or knowledge, is not for having power or subduing. It is for enjoying, for seeing, for judging, for salvation, and so on—that is, it is for attaining human fullness, as most traditions put it. Knowledge is for being.

We may not, we cannot, underestimate the value of reason. The sentence "Man is a rational animal" is used for the first time, as far as we know, by Aristotle. Translated into Latin it loses its meaning. Translated into vernacular languages it changes its sense. Aristotle's original phrase says rather that "Man, among the animals, is the one in whom language goes through."[21]

Logos passes by way of Man, and Man is not its sovereign. But if *logos* is translated as "rational animal," then it is *ratio* (Lat., reason) that becomes a human weapon. Animals have strength, horns, hides, hooves, and so on. Man has reason. We, too, are an armed animal. And Man, this armed animal, has conquered the others, has conquered matter, has built the atomic bomb, and so on. But victory does not lead to peace.

The disarmament of reason is a deep and difficult task. But we must undertake it if we hope to achieve true peace. No, the task is not easy. We have heard it said repeatedly that reason should be our guide, that we should be suspicious of feelings and sentiment, and that the alternative is to fall into irrationality.[22] That human reason, in all its frailty and limitations, has the power to challenge Man's actions and thoughts in no way means that it has the role of guide, let alone of inspirer, of human life. As happens in these cases, the difficulty lies in the choice of alternatives. Fideism, inspiration, feelings, and revelations have sufficiently shown their inability to rule human destinies. A pure voluntarism would be worse, evidently. We have no wish to disarm our reason only to fall victim to these superstitions.

To speak of a pure heart, and to adopt a Spinozan ethics, will always be a very rational thing to do. And to empty the heart in order to allow room for faith, in conformity with good Kantian intentions, leads us ultimately to the Hegelian reaction. Perhaps we have listened too little to Hamann and Jacobi to be able to follow the thread of European history in recent centuries. But the current situation has changed.

The cultural project of these last six thousand years must change. We must learn to overcome the "inertia of the mind." This will be the last obstacle in our considerations.

EVOLUTIONISTIC COSMOLOGY

I think that it must be clear by now that reflections on peace cannot be limited to finding ways of human fellowship and means to avoid war. For this, a world police officer would suffice. A reflection on peace leads us to the furthest depths of the very structure of reality. Peace is not the outcome of a strategy, but a fruit of contemplation.

Let us simplify the question to the maximum. Why would peace be impossible in a technological civilization? Why should the world of machines, which has integrated Man into itself, be less peaceful than the other three worlds? Would not a mechanical world, with its laws, be more suited for peace than the anarchical world of Men, the chaotic world of Nature, and the mysterious world of the Divinity?

We have already alluded to the theory of evolution as an epistemological presupposition. It is not so much a matter of the evolution of species as it is of the entire evolution of the universe. If reality is no more than the evolutionary process of an amorphous mass that gradually comes alive, becomes humanized, and even becomes divinized; if the human intellect, in its broadest and deepest sense, is no more than an evolutionary epiphenomenon affording us an awareness of what surrounds us; in a word, if there is no transcendence, no verticality, no "other dimension"; if everything that "there is" is only what evolves, then "peace" is an anachronistic word, and a sentimental residue that stirs a reaction on our part, just as we hear the cry of the living beings who are caught in the backwaters and blind alleys of the evolutionary sweep, and who do not share in the victors' banquet, who are not part of the evolutionary thread leading to "point Omega." The doctrine of universal evolution tells us that every step from one form of existence to another is taken at the cost of millions of beings who disappear in order that, out of their magma, inorganic, organic, living, sensate, and intelligent matter may rise up, heading for the superman and the divine. Experience teaches us that this is indeed the way things are in the world of Man. Out of thousands of slaves arises a handful of free persons; out of a human mass of millions emerge noteworthy personalities; and out of billions of people of the Third World sacrificed on the altars of progress will emerge a purified humanity, ready for the leap to the superman. Peace, then, would be the recognition of this evolution. Let us see to it that there be no racism, nationalism, or fanaticism, since these are not the values that will survive. Technocentrism is the victor. Those who know how to run machines will survive. The true peace is the one preached by the first God of Israel: peace for the people of God, the good, the winners. Nietzsche saw it clearly, although he seems then to have been crushed by his vision.

For centuries, a goodly part of humanity has journeyed with this more or less explicit goal. But we also know how far this competitive attitude can take us. Perhaps we are now beginning to realize, by their results, that all of these dreams have left out another ingredient of reality, one irreducible to the technocratic world. It may even be God, perhaps as an antidote, the most powerful symbol, although possibly the least adequate one. The Gods, generally speaking, have been Gods of war. *Yahweh saba'oth* is the God of armies. But there is no reason for the divine to be identified with an anthropomorphic God, "Lord" of history or "King" of the universe. A uniquely transcendent God, a God stationed only at the end of history, time, or the universe, has, generally speaking, been the belligerent God of many religions, despite the protests of the mystics and the refinements of the philosophers. This eschatological God, who receives only the few victors who have reached the goal, is a God not of peace but of war. Here is the God of evolution. Few are the saved. Some christians (including catholics) speak of a "perverse God."[23] But there is another possible conception of the Deity: a divinity who is neither only at the end nor only at the beginning, but who is in each and all of the moments of the temporal flux, who is immanent to all and transcends all—a Divinity who is not a Supreme Being but that Mystery of Being, that dimension of Reality, that we ourselves certainly are not, who is above us, but also below, and even within us—in Saint Augustine's oft-repeated phrase *"intimior intimo meo"* (deeper within me than my inmost depths).

If there is a divine splendor in Man, then a person cannot be a mere link in a chain that will one day produce the superman, or that will arrive at "point Omega." If Man has personal dignity in himself, and not as a mere means for a "higher" end, then human life must have a possible, and full, meaning for the person who lives it. The dilemma is an ultimate one: either peace or war—either the possible harmony that enables everybody to discover and live what the Gospels call *everlasting life,* or the war rooted in the very foundation of reality. One must scale the peak of the pyramid or resign oneself to being cannon fodder, an exploited laborer, *massa damnata,* so that construction can move ahead.

Both ways are open. Henry IV may have been right when he said, "Paris is well worth a mass," or perhaps Hitler was not so wrong, or those who dropped the atomic bomb! Perhaps peace is Man's last illusion, and we must open our eyes to the reality described by Kautilya, Machiavelli, Hobbes, Nietzsche, and so many others.

We have spoken above of a fundamental option, and have indicated that, up to a certain point, that option is in our hands. And it is here that liberation theology's renowned "option for the poor" wins a meaning for cosmic history that frequently has gone unrecognized. Such an option for the suffering element of humanity, on the part of those who have not been oppressed to the same extent, expresses a human solidarity of planetary proportions. We are not talking bourgeoisie or Marxism here, although these two words are capable of revealing something of the profound nucleus which we should like to discover. It is a matter of challenging the evolutionistic cosmology, which seems to posit that, for the evolution of the species up to *homo technologicus* (*et telematicus*), a "natural selection" is required (in this case an artificial one—or cultural, if you will) that will automatically eliminate those we have called "poor," who are also called—significantly and sarcastically—"underdeveloped" because they have not been integrated into the rising movement toward the tip of the developmental pyramid, which can only be reached by the few.

Philosophical reflection still arises from Aristotelian "wonderment" or Vedantic "disillusionment." But things go the other way too. What "wonderment" at the contrast between what *is* (exploitation, "natural selection," and so on) and what the human being thinks, dreams, and projects that *ought to be* (a human history distinct from the cosmic evolution)! What "disillusionment" at the sight of human suffering, since in Man a divine nucleus (the *ātman*) has been discovered that which walks in the opposite direction to the "illusion" of a false appearance (*samsāric*) of things!

The option for the poor is tantamount to our rebellion in the face of all the blind forces of nature and history.[24] "Do you think that when the 'Son of Man' comes he will find peace on earth?"[25]

Perhaps it is now understandable why the quest for peace requires a cultural disarmament in greater breadth than the one we had originally proposed.

It is here, then, that a basic reflection on the problem of peace leads us to disquieting questions, which we must resolve first of all in ourselves, in order to be able to come to be seed—free agents—of a new project, cosmic, human, and divine, for the moment in which we live.

The problem of peace is a human question, and therefore a real one. Its very difficulty instills a serene joy, for it enables us, at least at the individual level, to live the real and not the fictitious.

9 Pathways to Peace

Keeping faithful to the title of this study, let us take one last step in its interpretation. Up until now we have been referring to a disarmament of the dominant culture, to a conversion of modern culture into a culture of peace and not war. But, although competitive aggressivity is a modern specialty, warlikeness is no monopoly of technocratic culture. Most cultures that have survived have frequently transgressed the principles of peace. Can it be that peaceful civilizations have been barred from history with impunity? We have said above that it is not a matter of idealizing the past, or seeking to return to it. While many of the wars of other cultures are predominantly ritual, the great empires of antiquity, on practically all continents, have practiced war, and have not been regimes of *pax humana*. Accordingly, the disarmament we proclaim is much more radical than a mere reduction of modern civilization's degree of bellicosity. We have spoken of "transformation," of "metamorphosis." Our consideration is a more far-reaching one. And just because it is ambitious, it must be humble—clinging to the earth (*humus*) and Man (*homo*). Our perspective intends to embrace the experience of this historical Man. Thus, after an appeal to the past in the first section of this chapter, we shall return to the present in the two concluding sections.

LESSONS FROM HISTORY

The current human situation is very serious, and the historical failures underlying it are sufficiently eloquent to justify these parameters.

It is the actual historical experience of humanity on which we must pass judgment. What is there, or what has there been, in historical Man, that has created war as an institution? What confidence can we have in a society of states that spends an annual average of $30,000 per soldier and $500 per student?[1] When we realize that prehistoric men, who felt threatened by nature, have given birth to historical Man, who has finally placed the life of the planet at risk, we can— and must—wonder about "historical Man" project itself, and get hold of its six thousand years' experience.

This means that the *magistra vitae,* life as our teacher, not only invites us to extract teachings from historical occurrences in particular, but teaches us that the moment has arrived to challenge the historical myth itself, across the board. The problem is the myth of history: whether the historical constitutes Man exhaustively. And this, not because there is something beyond history, but because Man, even in his "hereness," is more than a historical being.

But lest we abandon the star that guides us in this pilgrimage, let us begin with the historical observation that we have repeatedly stated. Victory never leads to peace. Peace is not the fruit of victory.[2] This thesis can be defended from a philosophical viewpoint and from a historical viewpoint. To the latter purpose, we possess documents that surely must figure among the most instructive in all the history of humanity, ignored though they may be: the documents known as peace treaties, from Hammurabi down to our own day. We possess some eight thousand historical documents testifying to the optimism of the victors when it comes to establishing *their* peace. All of them, naively and tragically, chant the same refrain: "Now at last we shall have peace." And they repeat that "this is the war that will end all wars." It is as if they wished to do away with history *historically.* And before the ink or clay is dry, their neighbors' cannons or spears swing round to contradict these declarations.[3]

These documents demonstrate the greatest human blindness that can be imagined, but also the greatest naiveté. The thing that is now going to do away with wars is the "atomic deterrent," or "Star Wars," or the "new world order" based on the ideologies of a single victorious—and rootless—culture. One forgets that the vanquished (they themselves, their descendants, or the archetypes buried in the human subsoil) will rise up to settle accounts, and war will start all over again. We need only think of the American Indians, the Kurds, the Basques, the Jews, the Palestinians, and so on, throughout history. Let us repeat: victory never leads to peace. Victory leads to victory.

Even in the great mythologies of practically the whole world, the victory of the good (be they the Gods, or God, or believers) over evil never leads to peace. The road to peace is not victory, not even peaceful victory.

Thus, if we would make a serious meditation on peace, this is the level at which we must begin.

There is no question of denying the goodwill of the victors, although some treaties have been terribly cruel. It is not only Hammurabi who slaughtered the vanquished. We read Article 22 of the Treaty of Versailles, and we wonder how it is possible for that to have been written in 1918–19.[4] I repeat, a consideration on peace must study the experience that humanity has had in these last six or seven thousand years.

History shows us that victory has never led to peace, despite the efforts, goodwill, and conviction of those who defeated the Nazis, the Carthaginians, the Assyrians, or those "wicked folk who invaded us"! Peace has never been attained in this fashion.[5]

It seems irresponsible, after six thousand years of historical experience, to be unwilling to pose once more the uncomfortable question of whether civilization itself might be off course. But if at this historical moment, *we* do not have the intellectual capacity and spiritual strength to pose the problem at this level, I doubt that we shall be worthy of being called "intellectuals," "thinkers," or "responsible."

Einstein's remark rings in our ears: "With the splitting of the atom, everything has changed except the way we think." For years, I have been searching for the law of the inertia of the mind. The inertia of matter—since Kepler, Newton, and Einstein—can be more or less calculated. The inertia of the mind is much more ponderous. We continue to think, in science and history, in anachronistic categories that do not correspond to the current situation. Need all human civilization be warlike?

Surely we have improved a bit.[6] Less than a century ago, one in every four Africans was a slave.[7] Prisoners are no longer killed, although one can imagine what future generations in Iraq will think, who will not know about Saddam Hussein but who will have to suffer the consequences of the blockade and the defeat. To be sure, there are humanitarian laws and institutions that are intended to "soften the horrors of war." But, although Plautus's *vae victis!* is no longer popular, we still have not welcomed the vanquished themselves at the round table of peace instead of in the dock of the accused. If we did, then perhaps we should see that if this is the way wars end, then it is not worth the trouble to start them. And they would not get started. The sentencing of enemies, and passing

95

judgment upon them, belong precisely to the attempted justification of the war. But should we not have to learn from the last six thousand years of human experience? Peace is not attained by war.

What behooves us now is not to criticize peace treaties or to try to "humanize" war as much as we can. What behooves us now is to wonder about the way of thinking and the accepted institutions that have led us to this state of affairs. To reply that "this is the way things have always been" reveals that we have failed to understand either the seriousness of the current situation or the mutation to which humanity is being summoned. Peace is not achieved through a treaty, just as love is not reached by decree. There is something in the nature of peace, just as in that of love, that is withdrawn from commandment. A whole view of reality in general, and of Man in particular, is at stake.

It is not a matter of making the human being an angel. (Of course, the angels, too, waged war.) But neither is it a matter of cowering behind the shield of original sin and thinking that war is inevitable because we are sinners. We have recommended eliminating armies, not police. We have suggested the possibility of doing away with automatic means of destruction, not with spears and swords as effective symbols of authority. It is a matter of striking a middle course between the belief that Man is good (so that anarchism will be the answer) and the belief that Man is bad (and that one must defend oneself at all cost). Let us not forget that the *culture of certitude,* inaugurated in the West by Descartes, leads logically to a *civilization of security*—modern society's prevailing ideology. To live in insecurity and uncertainty is intolerable for rationality, but it is even pleasant in love. Saint Augustine calls peace the *incertum bonum* (the uncertain good).[8] It is better to place one's trust in reality—which to a large extent means placing it in ourselves—than to place it in our powerful "betters." "Quis custodiet ipsos custodes?" Who will watch the watchers?

We entertain these considerations in order to indicate how far cultural disarmament goes beyond a readiness to listen and to be tolerant. The disarmament to which the world situation urges us, under pain of apocalyptic catastrophe, is a cultural mutation at which the wisest persons of our era are already pointing.

RECONCILIATION

If it is not victory that leads us to the attainment of peace, what will enable us to find it? Here we repeat our last *sūtra:* Only reconciliation leads to peace.

"Reconciliation" is a word that, as we know, comes from *concilium*, and is akin to *ecclesia*, denoting the convocation of others. Reconciliation means convoking everyone, speaking with others.[9]

Reconciliation itself presents a tripartite structure. First there are the two parties in confrontation: male/female, right/left, rich/poor, catholics/protestants, believers/nonbelievers, capitalists/noncapitalists, whites/blacks, introverts/extroverts, and so on. But there is a third "party," as well, which is the object of the dispute, the bone of contention: a child, reason, territory, power, truth, or anything else. Here we find ourselves faced with a triadic configuration, with two possibilities for a solution.

The Scapegoat

The exceedingly old theory of the scapegoat seems to me to fall short.[10] (The scapegoat may be Poland, or Abyssinia, or a child in a divorce, or money, or the like.) The scapegoat does not solve the problem. The scapegoat is a provisional item, used by the rival parties until it is completely eliminated. (Will for instance Japan be the scapegoat between Europe and the United States?) A scapegoat serves for the moment: "We'll keep quiet about what's going on in Afghanistan or Poland, and you stop your maneuvering in Nicaragua or Chile." And so on.

This procedure does not lead to solutions, because the scapegoat cannot be totally annihilated. And then our first principle applies: neither does victory over the scapegoat ever lead to peace. The crucified rise again.

The blacks of Africa have been scapegoats for centuries. We need only think of Bartolomé de Las Casas, and that historic, fantastic tragedy in which, out of mercy toward the American Indians, between fifteen and forty-five million African blacks—20 percent of whom died en route—were brought over to work in place of the Indians. Charles V's laws of 1542 on human rights are among the most perfect ever promulgated. But they availed little, because the mighty found ways to sidestep them.

The pact struck between the powerful—Herod and Pilate, for example—by murdering a third party does not lead to peace. The problem is not solved. The problem is still on its feet, goading the conquerors and refusing to leave them in peace. It cannot be forgotten, and continues to act as if nothing had happened. History, too, has a memory. There is a law of *karma:* we cannot kill, crucify, conquer, and eliminate others, and afterward think that we are at peace. This is an ultimate, fundamental problem.

97

It is also a religious problem. Reconciliation cannot occur when we rely on a third party, even if this third party is not a person.

A current example, a grave and tragic one, is precisely our current scapegoat: matter (the earth in general and the atom in particular). Our era has perpetrated what I call a "cosmic abortion" or "cosmic violation." I use this expression in order to place in evidence the extent to which the modern West has lost its sensitivity. We are extremely sensitive to a mother's physiological abortion, which, of course, is an extremely serious problem. But who in the West has had the sensitivity—despite the cry of nearly all of the world's cultures, which we seek to marginalize as "folklore"—to perceive that to open the womb of matter (to split the atom) is a cosmic abortion of catastrophic proportions? We are cutting ourselves off more and more from the rest of the world, including animals. We have lost the sensitivity for communication. The atom is the scapegoat we use to maintain our standard of living. We have need of more energy, because we have shattered the rhythms of the earth. For every Italian (here the statistics are known) there is a ton of nuclear waste. And if Chernobyl warns us of a danger, then we shall think up a power plant that is a little more secure. This is the technocratic mentality: to look for solutions without ever going to the causes. Thus, it appears that no one truly wishes to denounce the cosmic abortion that represents a crime of *lèse-terre,* a crime of offense to the earth. We declare war on earth, and pretend that there is peace among peoples. Matter, too, rises again. Peace is a cosmic reality, as well.

To think only of solutions of security is to repeat once more the reaction that we have found in the peace treaties: the one with the sword is opposed by a spear, and the one who wields a simple shield, by a more complicated one; the one with a first-alert system is opposed by an electronic jammer; a missile with one warhead, by one with a dozen; when criminality is on the wax, more police; and so on and on. But peace is not attained in this way.

This is the mechanistic schema of thinking—the hydraulic schema, we might say (we have to bring the water level back up)—thereupon reinforced by the physical law of action and reaction. In this schema, "Do it and you'll pay for it." Here is the *lex talionis,* the law of retaliation, the law of the reestablishment of order on the basis of inflicting equivalent injury.

It is significant that this manner of thinking, in its Hebrew and Roman forms, prevailed for centuries in christian theology, in spite of the Sermon on the Mount and the doctrines of the Teacher of Nazareth. We are referring not only to canon law or the history of the church, but to the "talionistic" interpretation of one of the most fundamental christian dogmas: the "Redemption." A God who is the agent of distributive justice, and the simple custodian of a Supreme Law, requires reparation and restitution for the disobedience that has violated order and transgressed commandment. God hands over Jesus to be the vicarious victim for all humanity. He is the scapegoat. The debt must be paid.[11]

Transcendency

The other possibility likewise acknowledges the three elements. But here, the third element is not of a lower order (the expiatory victim). It is of a higher one (acknowledgment of transcendency). The two rival parties agree, not to pay a price, or to avenge themselves on a third party, but to forgive. Forgiveness is unintelligible in the mechanistic schema of thinking. This second possibility might perhaps be called a "vitalistic schema." If a sheep has been stolen, it can be returned. If a conquest has occurred, restitution can be made. But if a child has died, the parents cannot be compensated. And if innocence has been lost, it cannot be recovered. The punishment of the guilty party does not satisfy for sin. Only forgiveness erases sin.

But in order to have forgiveness, there must be the active or passive intervention of this third element, which transcends the conflictive situation. It would be tempting here to perform an exegesis of one of the christian texts that speaks most explicitly of peace. Were we to have meditated upon it more, not only would the Redemption have acquired another meaning, but the relationship between christianity and other religions would have adopted a more irenic face. We mean the text of John on the risen Christ. When Jesus appears to his disciples after the Resurrection, he gives them peace—and at once breathes into them the Holy Spirit, and as the fruit of this same divine Spirit tells them that in virtue of it they will be able to forgive or not forgive.[12] For reconciliation, there must be this third energy.

Strictly speaking, the dialectic of forgiveness is a trialectic. No one can simply forgive another person. This would be to arrogate to oneself a superiority that would only constitute a new affront to the "enemy." Forgiveness can be mutual only when the source of the forgiveness is transcendent to those who have offended one another, or who struggle with one another. The emperor can see to the reconciliation of two kings in combat; but no sovereign state can forgive an equally sovereign state. Such forgiveness can neither be given nor accepted. No international organization, agreement, or "peace-keeping force" can guarantee peace, unless some type of supranational authority is accepted. This is one of our current problems. Individuals and families can also forgive when they acknowledge a higher instance. Sovereign states must proclaim themselves "infallible" where their high sovereignty is concerned. An increasing awareness of supranational rights, and of crimes against humanity, opens the door to a more lasting state of peace. Democracy cannot justify or dictate everything.

This awareness cannot be the result of an accord struck by a given number of states. It must arise spontaneously as a myth accepted by all. There is no need of special laws or military vigilance in order not to practice cannibalism. And if slavery were once more to be institutionalized somewhere, a certain universal consensus would condemn such an act.

We have an example of this transcendency (unacknowledged by President Bush when he declared, on the eve of the 1992 Conference of Rio de Janeiro, that he was not going to put ecological questions ahead of "national interests") in the ecological awareness that is spreading across humanity. A third instance, the earth, is at hand, superior to the particular interests of particular nations or industries. And the word "superior" indicates that it is also to the benefit of the warring parties to acknowledge the third instance. On these grounds, I have taken the liberty of coining the word "ecosophy" to denote the wisdom of the earth itself. In true reconciliation, there are neither victors nor vanquished. All come out winners, because the whole, of which we make up a part, is respected. Unfortunately, our times have neglected education in forgiveness and reconciliation. The right to reconciliation is a human right. Man has a right to forgiveness.[13] Justice is more than a mere series of rules for maintaining a status quo.[14]

What we have been saying is in no way meant to suggest a merely sentimental conception of forgiveness. Forgiveness is not opposed to justice, but is an integral part of it. Justice does not consist in returning to the *status quo ante,* as if reality were not living and dynamic. Justice is not "redemption," but "renewal," as we have said. Accordingly, in the political order, justice is not simply making the guilty party pay or punishing transgressors. It is also the creation of a new order of things.[15]

DIALOGUE

How is reconciliation achieved? I should like to use a word that has become very popular nowadays: "dialogue." And of course I mean dialogue with the other, with the "enemy." But I do not mean a dialectical dialogue. Rather I have in mind what I have called "dialogical dialogue."[16] One must tirelessly pursue efforts to speak, to understand, and to make oneself understood, in order to open oneself to dialogical existence. What happens here is akin to what occurs with the alcoholic. His problem is not drinking, but not being able to want not to drink. The problem is not the "enemy," but not being able to want to deal with them. The interruption of dialogue is solipsism and death, because life itself is an ongoing dialogical dialogue. The other party always has something to say. I am not the only window on the world. Nor does my "I" exist without a "you" and the whole gamut of personal pronouns.

Dialogue is a science as well as an art. It involves the science of knowing both oneself (including what one thinks and wants) and the other. It is the science that knows that neither of these two cognitions is exhaustive, neither in myself nor in the other. Dialogue is a very much neglected science in our days, in which the *trivium* of classical education has come to be looked down on as "trivial." Education for peace spans the whole classical education in thinking, speaking, and reasoning—logic (dialectics), grammar, and rhetoric. Someone closed to dialogue can be as good a strategist and as astute as one could wish, but generally speaking is illiterate when it comes to the trivium. He doesn't know how to speak or discuss or, ultimately, to think, regardless of the number of his calculations and forecasts. We have already alluded to how underdeveloped is the cultural level of the "developed countries."

But dialogue is not only a science, it is also an art, a doing, an activity, a praxis. We have already referred to the ludic nature, the "playing" character, of the human being, and to the fact that the human game par excellence is the one we play with language. Conversation involves not only being "well versed" (well "turned")—in something, it also means "versing" to the other, "turning" to the other in order to find a "vertical" in which we may "con-verge" without "sub-version" or "per-version" of any kind, because thus we shall be "ad-verted" not to be "in-vertebrates" and thereby remain capable of "tra-versing" any "re-versal" that might "tergi-versate" our "di-vergencies." But let us not fall victim to any "vertiginous" "vertigo" here. Are we trying to be funny? Well, without humor there is scant hope for peace, either for the individual or for humanity.

A great deal has been written in our days on the "intercultural dialogue." And although much has improved, the table of dialogue has not generally been a round table. Let us not forget that the title

101

of the legendary King Arthur was *Dux bellorum,* and that only his knights were admitted to the illustrious table (which was round lest anyone have the "pre-sidency," the "fore-sitting"). It has been too hastily supposed that "other" cultures ought to come to *our* table, where we eat with the knife of dollars and the English fork, on the tablecloth of democracy (understood our way), on plates served up by the state, drinking the wine of progress and using the spoons (baby spoons, more recently) of technological development, while we sit on the chairs of history. I do not thereby wish to say that dialogue should be conducted seated on the floor, eating with our hands, drinking only water, and speaking gobbledygook. But I do say that it is a fundamental mistake to try to get everyone to sit at one table, and of course the Anglo-Saxon (among other names for it) is the most practical. What we need are "duologues" that are thereupon transformed into "multiloquies" among the various peoples of the earth (each with their neighbor, to begin with). Selling goods at a "single price" may have its advantages; but the myth of the single model ought to be demythologized. The modern mentality, of scientific coinage, has atrophied our sense of the uniqueness of every being and every situation. Dialogue is not a multitudinarious "meeting" at which only those speak who have a loud voice and know demagogy. Dialogue is a human act, on a human scale and with a human voice, in which men forge their humanness by discussing with words their divergencies.

Perhaps, before sitting down to the tables, we ought to "pray"— invoke something higher, which unites us—thereby acknowledging some transcendency which precisely makes us equally worthy, and which will enable us to find the right language for each case.

For all of this, wisdom is needed. Wisdom is the art that transforms destructive tensions into creative polarities, and this not by strategy, in order to "get our share," but because this polarity constitutes the very essence of reality. Polarity is not dualism, is not binary—since it is not governed by the dialectic of contradiction between the two poles, becasue each pole presupposes the other. Polarity is trinitarian. Otherwise the two poles would cease to be poles: they would fuse together or totally separate. This is what occurs in dialogal dialogue among persons, since nobody is a self-sufficient monad. Dialogical dialogue is not dialogue for reaching a solution, but is dialogue for being, since I am not without the other. "Esse est co-esse."

What this comes down to is: despite all obstacles, the road to peace consists in wanting to walk it. The desire for peace is pacifying in itself. The desire for peace is equivalent to a desire for dialogue, and the desire for dialogue arises when we think that we can learn something from others, along with converting them to our point of view where possible. Fanaticisms and absolutisms prevent persons from traveling together, because they make us believe ourselves self-sufficient or in full possession of the truth. "Si vis pacem, para teipsum" (Would you have peace? Prepare yourself).

Notes

The following abbreviations are used: *AV* (*Atharva Veda*); *BG* (*Bhagavad Gītā*); *MB* (*Mahābhārata*); *PL* (Migne, *Patrologia Latina*); *RV* (*Rig Veda*); *ST* (Aquinas, *Summa Theologiae*).

PREFACE

1. Quoted in Azad 1952, 1:28.

CHAPTER 1. THE MYTH OF PEACE

1. The core of this book consists of the address of the same title I delivered to the Antonio Machado Foundation of Madrid, for which I was awarded the first Antonio Machado Prize, bestowed by the Foundation in 1990.

CHAPTER 2. RECEIVING PEACE

1. This chapter reproduces certain paragraphs from my acceptance speech after the conferral of the Antonio Machado Prize, delivered in the Rector's Hall of the University of Alcalá de Henares on June 6, 1991.

CHAPTER 3. TOWARD A PHILOSOPHY OF PEACE

1. This chapter is a translation of some pages I wrote in an expression of gratitude for a volume published in my honor: Siguán 1989.

Although some points have already been made, or are mentioned again, it seems to me that this introductory summary will be helpful for an overview of the problem.

PART 2. THE RELIGIOUS DIMENSION OF POLITICAL PEACE

1. Our translation of this epigraph (from the Our Father of Matt. 6:10) reverses the syntax of the Greek not in order to contradict the original, but only to emphasize the nondualistic aspect of the Incarnation and reality.

2. Cf. my concept of ecosophy, in Panikkar 1991/48 and 1993/XXXIV.

3. Cf. Panikkar 1993/XXXIII.

CHAPTER 4. RELIGIOUS PEACE AND INTERCULTURAL DIALOGUE

1. Cf., for example, Schwally 1901, and the sequel to this work by Schmid 1974, especially in the chapter, "Heiliger Krieg und Gottesfrieden im Alten Testament," pp. 91–120.

2. Cf. Galtung 1987, which begins with a quotation from North American President Taft. In 1912, Taft justified his intervention in Mexico with the statement that the government of that nation should understand that "there is a God in Israel and he is on duty." Since then all of the Presidents through Bush have used a similar language.

3. The long-awaited pastoral letter of the bishops of the United States on war, despite the criticisms set forth vis-à-vis their country's military policy, does not even dare condemn the possession of nuclear arms as a deterrent, despite the declarations of Vatican II.

4. Cf. the documents collected in Peña 1982, where the author describes the enormous success of the "Vitorian doubt." Francisco de Vitoria managed to assuage the doubts of the Spanish conscience with respect to the moral rectitude of the conquest of America, and to have Charles V hand down the laws of 1542 guaranteeing the Indians all of their human rights and prohibiting the waging of war against them. Cf. also the clear position of the same Juan de la Peña in his *De Bello contra Insulanos*.

5. Cf. the classification of wars as "ethnic," "imperial," and "religious" in Panunzio 1982, p. 34.

6. Cf. "Das lateinische *bonus* glaube ich als 'den Krieger' auslegen zu dürfen; vorausgesetzt, dass ich mit Recht *bonus* auf ein älteres *duonus* erhalten rückführe (vergleiche *bellum; duellum;* worin mir jenes *duonus* erhalten scheint). *Bonus* somit als Mann des Zwistes, der Entzweiung (*duo*) als Kriegsmann" (I believe I can explain the Latin *bonus* as "the warrior"—provided I am correct in understanding *bonus* as coming from an older *duonus*. Compare *bellum,* from *duellum,* on which analogy I

conjecture to the existence of an earlier *duonus*. Thus, *bonus* as the man of contention, of the "twist," of the falling out, of the sundering-in-two [*duo*] as the man of war.) (Friedrich Nietzsche, *Zur Genealogie der Moral*, I, 5; quoted by Schlechta edition of 1966, 2:777.)

7. Cf. Heer 1953 and 1980 for overwhelming data.

8. This phenomenon can still be observed today in Papua New Guinea, where war is ritual recreation. This factor, missing in modern technological wars, points to the mutation of the warrior, as we shall indicate below.

9. In "contemporary democracies," *authority* is vested in the people, who delegate it to their civil representatives. These in turn are theoretically over those who hold military *power*.

10. The total cost of killing an "enemy" in Julius Caesar's time was $1.00. World War I had to pay $20,000. World War II, $115,000. And the Vietnam War cost $300,000 per dead enemy. In World War I, 90 percent of those killed were military; in World War II, 50 percent; and in the Vietnam War, only 10 percent (ninety percent of those killed were civilians). The Gulf War was even worse. (Data collected by Frank Barnaby of SIPRI, Stockholm.)

11. Cf. K. Geyer's bibliography on "Peace in the New Testament," in Liedke, vol. 9 (1972), pp. 187–99.

12. The *Enciclopedia Filosofica* (1979), under "Pace" (peace), offers a consideration of the relations between peace and political communities, and refers "to its opposite, war." About peace, it would seem, there is not much to be said.

13. *Salām:* habitual sign of the Muslim greeting, which includes peace with God and with one's sibling, along with well-being. Cf. *Qur'ān* 6:56. The Sumerian root *silim* (Accadian *sālamu*) indicates fullness, health, being, and being complete.

Shanti is the reflection and simultaneous projection of the inner harmony of the universe. For the Vedic tradition, cf. the texts and commentaries of Panikkar 1977/XXV, pp. 304ff.

For *shalom,* cf. Schmid 1971a. The same author treats the identical subject in 1971b.

The Greek *eirēnē* "designates first of all peace regarded as a lasting state (unlike Homer's *philotēs*, which concerns the striking of an accord); it is not originally a juridical or diplomatic term" (Chantraine 1968, under *eirēnē*).

The Latin word *pax* (*pacem a pactione*) has the expressly juridical meaning of "pact."

The Russian word *mir* means, at one and the same time, "peace" and "world"—the latter in the sense of *kosmos,* that is, the cosmos as beautiful, harmonious, orderly. It means looking at the world as it really is (ought to be): peaceful. The absence of peace destroys this world. It is the traditional idea of *ordo, ṛta,* and so forth.

14. Cf. Heer 1980, p. 43.

15. Cf. the beginning of the article "Pace," in the new *Dizionario Enciclopedico di Spiritualità,* 1975: "State of mind sprung from the supernatural unification of all human tendencies in the direction of a single ideal, . . . the fundamental fruit of charity." And, of course, "perfect peace is impossible in this life of struggles and toils."

16. Representing an extreme position, Coste writes: "Human peace and the peace of Christ are two problematics, two concerns, two different languages" (*Dictionnaire de Spiritualité,* 1983, under "Paix," col. 43). Thereupon, however, he modifies this extreme differentiation. The second contribution, by Sieben, treats, naturally, of "paix intérieur."

17. Cf. Janssen 1979, under "Friede," 2:543–91.

18. By way of example, I shall cite the fourth observation or admonition contained in the foreword of Miguel de Molinos's once so celebrated *Guía espiritual* (1675): "[This is] the subject of this book, which is to uproot the rebelliousness of our own will in order to achieve interior peace [the author at once quotes Hugo Cardinalis's commentary on Psalm 13: 'Haec est enim pax voluntatis nostrae, ut sit per omnia conformis voluntati divinae' (For this is the peace of our will, that it be in every way conformable to the divine will); and after citing Psalm 13 itself, 'Viam pacis non cognoverunt' (They have not known the way of peace), concludes this final preliminary observation with these words:] May the Lord be pleased to give me his divine light, in order to discover the secret paths of this interior journey and supreme felicity of perfect peace" (Molinos 1976, p. 118).

19. We could cite the aphorisms of Lao-tzu, Buddha, Isaiah, Confucius, Jesus, Muhammad, and so on, in this same tenor, although they ought not to be removed from their respective contexts.

20. Cf. Janssen 1979, pp. 547ff., with examples of what we are saying.

21. In July 1991, Cardinal Tarancón repeated, in the spring courses of the University of Alcalá in El Escorial that religion ought not to interfere in politics—an understandable and sound position in the recent Spanish context, provided "religion" be understood as "institutionalized catholic church" and "politics" as a likewise institutionalized "parliamentary game."

22. "Man erinnert sich an die Definition des Friedens in Dt. 20,10ff.; entweder freiwillige Unterwerfung oder gewaltsame Vernichtung." (One is reminded of the definition of peace given in Deut. 20:10ff.: either willing submission or violent annihilation.) (Schmid 1974, p. 108). The reader would do well to examine the passage from Deuteronomy.

23. It is significant that specialized institutions have once more, in the last decades, treated the subject of peace. To give just two different examples: the thematic title of the Twenty-fifth Eucharistic Congress, held at Barcelona in 1952, was: *Ipse est Pax nostra* ("It is he who is our peace," Eph. 2:14); cf. Acts of the Congress 1952. It was likewise the theme of the Congress of the Société Jean Bodin in 1958 (cf. Bodin 1958).

24. The proliferation of institutions dedicated to the propagation

and study of peace is a symptom, today, of the fact that the crisis has reached the knowledge of the masses. It is also a sign of hope. Cf., e.g., Keynes 1920, Institute for World Order 1981, Lücker 1980, Pestalozzi 1982, Cortesi 1985.

25. This book constitutes the complement and exemplification of another work of mine, Panikkar 1945/XL.

26. Cf. Panikkar 1978/1.

27. It is usually left out of consideration in statistical studies on poverty and "underdevelopment" that the "developed" model cannot serve as a model on a world scale. If the whole world had the same number of automobiles per capita or consumed the same quantity of paper or electricity as the developed countries, life on the planet would be ecologically inviable beyond the twenty-first century, speaking very optimistically. The average citizen of a developed country consumes fifty times as much energy as one of a moderately developed country. The arithmetic is easy: earth does not offer all this.

28. I recall the reaction of one of my most enlightened audiences, in Delhi, in 1989, at one of my "Ganguly Lectures," which bore precisely the title of the present volume, "Cultural Disarmament." India's neo-converts to modern technoscience as a panacea for all maladies, especially economic ones, did not receive my thesis with enthusiasm. It seemed to them at least inopportune (and I agreed with them from "their viewpoint"). The more "traditional" members of my audience observed that what classical Indian culture lacked was precisely reinforcement, and there were even those who championed the need to be armed against the cultural genocide to which they were being subjected (and I agreed with them as well, on condition that the reinvigoration in question could not be implemented by following the game rules of the dominant culture, nor by the exercise of violence).

29. Panikkar 1983/XXXIII.

30. The plenary meetings of the Global Forum for Human Survival (Oxford 1988, and Moscow 1991), which were attended by representatives of nearly every current culture, to the stupefaction of so many, expressed the practically unanimous opinion that, if the world continues along its present, modern path, it has no more than fifty years to live. Cf. Vittachi 1989.

31. According to the World Bank's "Bulletin on World Development" (Washington 1990), there are 1,116 million poor in the world, living on less than 3,000 pesetas a month. At the same time, many of the governments of such countries spend veritable fortunes in the purchase of weaponry: in 1987, India $3,200 million, Afghanistan $1,300 million, and Angola $1,600 million, again according to the World Bank. For an analysis of these and other data, cf. *Éxodo* (Madrid) May-June 1991, pp. 6ff.

32. Cf., by way of an informative example, Nebbia 1991, with its appended anthology. Cf. also Perroux 1983.

33. The recent colloquiums held under the auspices of UNESCO (1981, 1984a) reveal cracks in the monolithic block of development, but still attempt to salvage the concept.

34. Cf. Ladrière 1977.

35. Birou and Henry 1976 does so timidly; Vachon 1988, more explicitly; and Sachs 1992, radically. Cf. the recent international symposium, held under the auspices of the Institut Interculturel de Montréal, "Living with the Earth," Montreal 1993.

36. Cf. UNESCO 1984b.

37. Cf. Panikkar 1990/XXX.

38. In 1961 I introduced the term *Ummythologisierung,* connoting rather a reshaping than a replacement, and thus in contradistinction to Rudolf Bultmann's celebrated *Entmythologisierung.* Cf. Panikkar 1961/ 15. Cf. also Panikkar 1979/XXVII.

CHAPTER 5. POLITICAL AND RELIGIOUS PEACE

1. "In seiner philosophischen Bedeutung erst seit kurzem, in seinem Rang als Prinzip des Denkens und Handelns noch kaum wahrgenommen, gilt Friede, gleichwohl von den Anfängen der Geistesgeschichte an als fundamentales Menschheitsproblem, das als solches wiederholt zum Gegenstand thematischer Reflexion wurde," writes E. Bisser in Ritter 1972, under *Friede.* And indeed, neither Lalande 1980, nor Foulquié 1962, nor Ferrater Mora 1965 deals with the subject of the word "peace." As for Rosenthal and Yudin 1967, there is no place for "Peace," but only "Peaceful Coexistence" is mentioned. König 1956 mentions only "Friedensritualien," and Hastings 1917 has only two pages under "Peace," on the christian concept of peace. The 1974 *Encyclopaedia Britannica* does not have the word "Peace" in its *Macropedia.* And the *Micropedia* only has entries of minimal importance: "The Peace," "Peace Corps," "Peaceful Coexistence," "Peace Mission," "Peace of God and Truce of God," "Peace Pipe" (cross-reference), "Peace Policy, that is, "Grant's Peace Policy," and "Peace River" (twice). And all of this in two columns. The *Encyclopaedia Universalis* (1985) has a scant three pages on "Paix" ("Le maintien de la paix et le réglement des différends"). By contrast, the articles on "Guerre" (without counting "guerrilla") cover more than 51 pages (speaking, of course, of the World Wars and others).

2. "Social science has uncovered more knowledge about war than about peace, just as psychology probably has yielded more insights into negative deviance (such as mental illness) than into positive deviance (such as creativity)." Thus begins J. Galtung's article on the word "Peace" in Sils 1968.

3. Cf. Polanyi 1957, Heilbronner 1974, López de Romaña 1989, Rahnema 1991.

4. Without seeking to defend the drug traffic or "terrorism," we

must say that both phenomena—for very different reasons—are accepted by the defenders of the status quo as the culprits one can name of an anonymous, endemic, and far deeper evil. And these commentators do so not necessarily in bad faith, but by virtue of an intrinsic requirement of the system that it defend itself by shifting attention to problems that muster a greater consensus.

5. In other studies, I have attempted to document these assertions. Cf., among other sources, Panikkar 1982/17, 1982/18.

6. The arms race in "civilized" countries, like the number of prisoners there, pursues its ascending course. ($1,700,000 a minute in 1986. The advertising industry, however, does not lag far behind—in 1985, in the United States alone, it spent a million dollars a minute [*Time,* May 9, 1986].) The foreign debt of the most debt-ridden countries pursues its mind-boggling ascent. (The U.S. foreign debt, which was in the amount of $900 million in 1980, had risen to $2 billion in 1985. But from the beginning of World War II until 1982, the annual military expenditures of this same nation, adjusted for population increase, rose from $75 per capita to $855, according to Siward 1983.) According to Rodrigo Carazo Odio, former president of Costa Rica and in 1983 president of the United Nations University of Peace, "in the developing nations there is one soldier for every 250 inhabitants, but only one physician for every 3,700" (*Teilhard Review* 18 [1983]: 87).

7. Cf. Panikkar 1986/13.

8. Some random samples: The "new poor" of the First World (developed and wealthy) now number 100 million (Latouche 1991, p. 27), of whom 34 million are in the United States alone (2.1 million more than in 1988) (U.S. Census Bureau, 1991). The inequalities of the gross national product are growing by the day (in 1900, poor countries had a GNP equivalent to one-half of that of the rich countries; in 1970, the ratio was 1:20 in 1900 dollars or 1:40 in 1970 dollars (Barnet and Müller 1974, p. 190). From 1980 to 1988, the average GNP of the populations of Africa and Latin America had fallen by 15 percent (*L'Altra Pagina* 6 [1989]: 1). According to other data, from 1981 to 1990, in Latin America, the drop was 10.1 percent, which is practically the same (J. Cabrera Rivera, in Berten and Luneau 1991). The situation is not exclusively a Third World one: in 1984, one percent of property owners owned 50 percent of all the land in the United States, and one percent of farm owners were using 30.3 percent of the arable land (*Sojourners* 12 [1986]:13; Hart 1984), which is almost the same as in El Salvador, where one percent of the landholders own 57 percent of the land, although the situation is not comparable in view of the fact that in the Central American country there are no other opportunities (McGovern 1985, p. 105). On another level, in 1992 some 20 percent of the countries of the world shared 82.7 percent of the world's wealth, while another 20 percent held 11.7 percent. Simply by adding these sums together, one discovers that 40 percent of humanity owns 94.4 percent of

the wealth of the entire world (*Le Monde Diplomatique,* June 1992, p. 8; cited in the official organ of the United Nations, PNUD, 1992). And we could continue our citations. The situation goes back to the so-called "end of military colonialism" (Kennedy 1975).

9. Despite the efforts of journalists to emphasize the (for that matter, undeniable) importance of the *perestroika,* little will have been achieved in the long run if that "remodeling" is limited to a commercial and tourist-industry liberalization.

10. Compare the difference in the reactions of a warlike world to the parallel resolutions of the United Nations condemning, respectively, Israel and Iraq. Cf. the documents collected in Tribunal contra la Guerra del Golfo 1992.

11. It is significant that, in Adela Cortina's delicious description of an international symposium, in her chapter, "La ética contemporánea y los poderes de la tierra," there is not the faintest suggestion of a criticism of the actual structures of the technocratic system, and that everything is based on a search for solutions that will leave the taboo of scientific and technological civilization intact. Cf. Cortina 1991, pp. 114–31.

12. "Der Friedenszustand unter den Menschen, die nebeneinander leben, ist kein Naturzustand (*status naturalis*), der vielmehr ein Zustand des Krieges ist, d.i. wenngleich nicht immer ein Ausbruch der Feindseligkeiten, doch immerwährende Bedrohung mit demselben. Er muss also *gestiftet* werden." (The condition of peace among human beings who live next to one another is not a "natural state," a *status naturalis,* but rather a condition of war, that is, although not always an outbreak of hostilities, still a permanent threat of the same. It must therefore be *established.*) (Kant 1795, p. 18.)

13. Cf., among many other sources, Schell 1982.

14. Cf. Jaspers's grave warning in 1958 (Jaspers 1960, intro.): "Von der Drohung totaler Vernichtung sind wir zur Besinnung auf den Sinn unseres Dasein zurückgewiesen. . . . Als ein besonderes Problem kann die Atombombe nicht genügend erfasst werden. Nur wenn der Mensch als er selbst auf die in seine Hand gegebene Möglichkeit antwortet, kann er ihr gewachsen sein." (The threat of total annihilation impels us to come to our senses concerning the meaning of our being. . . . It is beyond one's grasp how special a problem the atom bomb is. Only when we human beings as such are willing to answer for the capability that we find in our hands, shall we be up to dealing with it.)

15. "We do not come to know history, which is an indissoluble mixture of nature and society, except in the process of transforming it and ourselves. As Vico put it so long ago, we really know only what we ourselves do. For people today truth is what we make, what we 'verify.' . . . Praxis that transforms history is not the degraded embodiment of some pure, well-conceived theory; instead it is the very matrix of all authentic knowledge, and the decisive proof of that knowledge is value" (Gustavo Gutiérrez, as quoted in B. Gibellini 1979, pp. 18–19).

16. Cf. Guthrie 1987.

17. Cf. *Dhammapāda,* IV, 8–9 (51–52); cf. also Matt. 23:3.

18. The whole of chapter 6 of Atīśa's *Bhodi-pathapradīpa* is devoted to the relationship between *prājnā* and *upāya* (theory and praxis). Cf. Sherburne's translation 1983, p. 130.

19. *Leggenda Perugina,* 74 (cited in Boff 1982, p. 36); cf. also John 3:2.

20. Understanding "sociology of knowledge" in the sense it has in the superb studies by Max Scheler and collaborators in Scheler 1924, followed by Mannheim 1964 and introduced in the North American world by Berger and Luckmann 1966.

21. Cf. Panikkar 1981/10 and 1983/11 (reprinted in 1993/ XXXIII). It goes without saying that this expression of mine has little to do with the later interpretation *pro domo Delphini,* popularized by F. Fukuyama.

22. Guardini had already discerned this situation in the 1940s. Cf. Guardini 1950.

23. "Friedensforschung ist notwendigerweise interdisziplinäre Forschung," admits W. Huber, in Ritter 1972, under "Friedensforschung" (Quest for Peace). But it has scarcely been taken into account, much less been taken seriously, that peace is also an intercultural subject.

24. Cf. my course "Religion, Revolution and Peace" at the University of California, which I hope to publish one day, along with my seminar on the various concepts of peace.

25. *Katha Upanishad,* I, 20.

26. Cf. Panikkar 1982/18.

27. Cf. Panikkar 1978/1.

28. For an analysis of the nine dimensions of all religion, cf. Panikkar 1965/IX, pp. 58–147.

29. The German word denoting peace, *Friede,* is etymologically related to *Freund* ("friend") and to *Freiheit* ("freedom"). Without freedom and friendship, there is no peace. The Sanskrit root is *pri-* (cf. *priya,* "beloved"; *prema,* "love"), and means, on the one hand, to "love," and on the other, to "care," to show solicitude. Without an active, real love there is no peace. Cf. Heidegger: "Das Wort Friede meint das Freien, das Frye, und fry bedeutet bewahrt vor Schaden und Bedrohung, bewahrt-vor, . . . d.h. geschont. Freien bedeutet eigentlich schonen. . . . Das eigentliche Schonen ist etwas *Positives* und geschieht dann, wenn wir etwas zum voraus in seinem Wesen belassen, wenn wir etwas eigens in sein Wesen zurückbergen, es entsprechend dem Wort freien: einfrieden" ("Bauen, Wohnen, Denken," in Heidegger 1967, 2:23).

30. Cf. Augustine, *De Civitate Dei,* XIX, 13, 1; cf. also: "Pax hominum est ordinata concordia" (ibid.; *PL* 41:640) and Thomas Aquinas's note *ST* II-II, q.29, a.1, ad 1.

31. The dynamic trait of peace has not been wholly forgotten in scholasticism. The accent falls not so much on *tranquillitas* as on *ordo,* which presupposes power and will.

32. Cf. Janssen 1979, pp. 553ff., with abundant citations.

33. "Friede ist ein Zustand innerhalb eines Systems grösserer Gruppen von Menschen, besonders von Nationen, bei dem keine organisierte, kollektive Anwendung der Drohung von Gewalt stattfindet" (J. Galtung, in E. Krippendorf 1968; quoted in W. Huber, "Friedensforschung," in Ritter 1972, p. 1120. Our conception of peace would accept all of this as the point of departure for a consideration of the subject more in depth.

34. Cf. Panikkar 1977/16, 1984/3.

CHAPTER 6. RELIGIOUS TRANSFORMATION OF POLITICAL PEACE

1. Cf. Horace, *Epist.* 1, 10, 24: "Naturam expelles, furca tamen usque recurret."
2. Cf. Panikkar 1978/1, of which the following paragraph is a summary.
3. "Man's life on earth is a waging of war" (Job 7:1, in the Vulgate).
4. Cf. Thomas Aquinas: The "pax imperfecta, quae habetur in hoc mundo," while it is a "true peace" is not the same as the *pax perfecta,* that of the other life (*ST* II-II, q.29, a.2, ad 4).
5. Cf. *BG* II, esp. 19–21.
6. This has gone so far that, in 1979, on catholic criteria, the *Enciclopedia Filosofica* could write, under the word "War": "War can be just or unjust, depending on whether its motive is just or unjust." And: "Today, the mighty progress of science and technology has produced such fearfully destructive means of war, that it would be utterly inappropriate, even in cases when it would be morally licit, to have recourse to war in order to avenge an 'offense.' " One must not forget—as W. Dignat recalls, in *Die Religion in Geschichte und Gegenwart* 1958, under the word, "Friedensbewegung" (Peace Movement), that as early as 1947, Cardinal Ottaviani had come out against war on the grounds that "modern war is qualitatively distinct from earlier wars." And this was actually the opinion of Pius XII. Cf. the astonishing assertions of Cardinal Lercaro at Vatican II: "With regard to weapons of indiscriminate destructive power (especially atomic, bacteriological, and chemical weapons), the Church ought not to limit itself, as does the schema [13, *Gaudium et Spes*], to decry their potential use, but rather ought henceforward to anticipate the judgment that the Lord will surely pronounce upon them at the end of human history: the possession of those weapons is a gigantic concentration of power and violence merely in itself, and confronts nations and their heads with an extremely proximate temptation to perpetrate the gravest delicts against all humanity. Therefore those weapons, merely in themselves, constitute an element of the diabolical, and are a temerarious assault against God. . . . Thus, the Church may not even temporarily ratify human discourse advocating the balance of terror, or positing so much as a provisional utility in the possession of those weapons for the immediate preservation of peace.

"Instead, the Church ought to tell all of the possessors of those arms that it is illicit to produce or stock them, and that they have the categorical obligation to proceed, absolutely and at once, without any delay of any kind, to the simultaneous and total destruction of them all" (Lercaro 1983, pp. 468–69).

As we know, the Council sought to be more "conciliatory," and did not *ex professo* condemn the possession of atomic weapons, which led the bishops of the United States to back down from their original condemnation. Cf. chap. 4, n. 3, above.

7. "Cuncta fecit bona in tempore suo et mundum tradidit disputationi [dispositioni] eorum" (Eccl. 3:11, in the Vulgate).

8. John 18:36.

9. All of this was well documented in its time. Cf., e.g., a clear, succinct summary in *Il Regno* (Bologna), vol. 27, no. 465/12 (June 15, 1982), pp. 265–66.

10. Cf. La Valle 1990, 1991.

11. Cf. Jean Bodin, as cited in Janssen 1979, p. 557.

12. Ibid. Hobbes's lamentably celebrated pronouncement, with its Machiavellian echoes, is "Auctoritas, non veritas fecit legem" (Authority, not truth, makes the law) (*Leviathan* 2:26).

13. In his review of Kant's *Zum ewigen Frieden*, quoted in Janssen 1979, p. 568.

14. I have been developing this concept since 1952, and have applied it to many cases. Cf. Panikkar 1963/V, 1971/XII, 1979/XXII.

15. Quoted in Janssen 1979, p. 569.

16. Cf. Panikkar 1984/26. It is to this question that I have devoted some of my recent studies, many of which are only on the point of publication, or even still in the manuscript stage.

17. "*Kratos* means neither 'physical strength' (*ischys, sthenos*), nor 'strength of soul' (*alkē*), but 'superiority, predominance,' whether over an assembly . . . . But in other uses, *krateros* is close in meaning to *krataios* ('hard, cruel'), *kratus* ('hard'). . . . *Kratos* is akin to the Indo-Iranian *kratu*, which denotes the magical *virtus* of the warrior." Thus runs the summary of the study on this word in Benveniste 1969, 2:71. I abstain from remarking, ironically and sorrowfully, that the magical strength of the machine has "prevailed" not only over *homo faber*, but also over *animal loquens*.

18. Cf. Panikkar 1967/XV. Later I found this thought frequently. Cf. R. Koselleck, "Erfahrung der Beschleunigung" (the experience of acceleration), as the "gemeinsamer Nenner" (the common denominator) of the present awareness of modernity, quoted in Grumbrecht 1979, 4:109. Cf. also the quotation from Benz, n. 24, below.

19. Cf. the book that caused such a sensation in its time, Philberth 1963. "Never before," it says, "has the danger existed that the earth, through the work of human beings, could be rendered impossible to live on," begins the pocketbook edition of 1964, p. 5.

20. The bibliography is incalculably extensive today. Cf., e.g., *Bulletin of Peace Proposals,* the organ of the International Research Institute (Oslo), and a number of the issues of the *UNESCO Courier* devoted to peace (or war, disarmament, etc.). The latter, in vol. 5, no. 48, of April 1982, describes "the peace movement: how it was, what it is, what it can be," especially in a German context. The same issue lists the headquarters of 2,300 similar movements throughout the world.

21. There is no one-hundred-percent-safe atomic system. Even discounting possible sabotage and war, the stockpiles of thousands of weapons and chemical and nuclear deposits on the planet threaten a catastrophe of world proportions within a few centuries. In terms of current statistics, which also include the human factor, before mid-century we shall have a nuclear catastrophe of continental dimensions. The role of Prometheus is not played with impunity.

22. This was intuited by Teilhard de Chardin, who made it the ruling consideration of his thought. He therefore taught a cosmic evolution that would reach a "point Omega" regardless of human folly. He took God and the cosmos very seriously, then—but not Man, who is a mere intermediate step in evolution.

23. Cf., e.g., Landgren-Baekstroem 1982. Things have grown far worse since then; and the hypocrisy of calling the selective sale of weapons to "friendly countries" by the name of "arms reduction" will unleash a ferocious counterrevolution. "You shall not prevail, 'Gideon'—you have too many people!" (cf. Judg. 7:21–22). United States policy will not win out—it requires too many "allies"!

24. "The fact that acceleration as a striking historical phenomenon only comes on the scene with Christianity indicates that it stands in a direct connection with the specifically christian understanding of time, history, and historicity," writes Benz 1978, p. 18. Acceleration, he is telling us, is a sign of the technological era, and has not sprung up on christian soil by coincidence. "Acceleration is an act of God's freedom in the drama of salvation history," he summarizes on p. 21.

25. This is the central thesis of my study, Panikkar 1984/26, cited above.

26. Cf. Panikkar 1986/14, where I suggest that the cancer of the individual microorganism corresponds to the cancer of the social macroorganism.

27. Cf., e.g., George 1976; Erler 1987.

28. Cf. my book, soon to appear, *Sacred Secularity.*

29. Cf. the ancient Egyptian *ahau* ('h'w), denoting duration in the beyond, which duration, properly speaking, is the time of life, so that the word was used of the afterlife as well as of the present one. Cf. Hornung 1978, p. 281 and passim. *Aiōn* is Greek, and *āyus,* Sanskrit.

30. We prescind from the theoretical theological problems that come up in discussion with traditional religions, since they do not come within the scope of this study.

31. The notorious *philia tou kosmou,* or "friendship with the world"

that is "enmity with God" of James 4:4 (cf. 1 John 2:15), ought to be interpreted, in the light of Matt. 6:24 ("No man can serve two masters"), as a call to transform the "system."

32. Cf. Panikkar 1979/XXII, 1975/1.

33. Doubtless we ought to refer here to Eliade 1949.

34. Cf. works as different as Weizsäcker 1984 and Hawking 1988. Both begin with the unexamined presupposition that the cosmos is a historical entity.

35. Cf. my forthcoming *La métapolitique*.

36. Cf. Panikkar 1984/20, which anticipates some of the ideas set forth here.

37. Panikkar 1988/20.

38. "Ordinata concordia": Augustine, *De Civitate Dei,* book 19, chaps. 12, 13, 14.

"Pax temporalis apparens": Thomas Aquinas, *ST* II, q.29, a.2.

"Pax imperfecta": When Luther thus internalized the concept of *pax spiritualis,* "he sundered the medieval connection between spiritual and worldly peace, relegating the latter to the status of a theologically indifferent outward peace, which was the affair not of Christians, but of jurists (whose role corresponded to that of the modern state)" (Janssen 1979, p. 559; cf. ibid., the apposite citations from Luther).

39. Few have expressed the traditional feeling with greater beauty, and overtones less masochistic, than has Saint John of the Cross:

> Withdraw me from this death,
> My God, and give me life!
> Hold me not entrammeled
> In this snare so taut!
> See how I long to behold Thee:
> My torment is so utter
> That I die because I die not!

(*Coplas del alma que pena por ver a Dios,* in Juan de la Cruz 1975, p. 391).

40. From this perspective, Pope John Paul II's obsession with abortion could be interpreted as a modern endorsement of secularity. If human fetuses went to heaven to enjoy the beatific union as perfect human beings, the Pope would have no reason to equivalate them with thousands of children—and adults—who die an unnatural death every day.

41. Cf. the article, "Gerechtigkeit," by J. M. Díez Alegría, in *Sacramentum Mundi* 1968, which is already a step in the direction of bridging this huge gap.

42. I must refer to a study of mine that has been finished for some time, but of which only fragments have appeared: "*Muktitattva.*"

43. Cf. Panikkar 1986/13, where an attempt is made to show their intrinsic relation, as humanity has known it since the most ancient Egyptian times.

44. Cf. Lücker 1980; cf. also the periodical *Dharma World*, and so many others.

45. "We believe that, as religious human beings, we have a special responsibility for the building of a peaceful world community, and that we can make a special contribution to it" (Lücker 1980, p. 21).

"We have all received from our faith the assignment to seek justice in the world, in a community of free persons enjoying equal rights" (Lücker 1980, p. 22)—words of the *Princeton Declaration* (September 7, 1979) at the Third World meeting. It was unanimously approved by 338 delegates from 47 nations.

"What is ultimately at stake is the salvation and integral fulfillment of the human being in the individual and social domain," said the president of the organization, Delhi (Catholic) Archbishop Angelo Fernandes (Lücker 1980, p. 67).

46. Cf. the summary of the Asian branch of this association, *Peace through Religion* 1976, with contributions of the principal religions of the continent, although in the absence of the "archaic" or "primitive" ones.

47. Cf. the Final Document, in UNESCO Documentation SS-79/ CONF. 607/10 of February 6, 1980.

48. Cf. Holl 1978.

49. Cf. the quarterly *Pax Christi International Bulletin* (Antwerp), e.g., no. 41 (August 15, 1982).

50. Cf. the discussion with the Russian Church at Zagorsk (March 1–21, 1982), and the various demonstrations against nuclear weapons, frequently regarded as an offense to God and immoral in themselves.

51. Cf. Edizioni Cultura della Pace of Santo Domenico de Fiesole, Florence, which has published nearly a score of volumes since 1989 and which is composing an entire *Enciclopedia della Pace*. This enormous task was undertaken on the initiative of recently deceased (in an automobile accident in 1992) Ernesto Balducci, of whom I wish to express my admiration and esteem. Cf. also *Papeles para la Paz*, a periodical published by Madrid's Centro de Investigación para la Paz; etc.

52. Cf. Job 16:22.

53. Cf. Matt. 18:6–7 and par.

54. Cf. *BG* I, 1.

55. The mysticism of all times has known this since the beginning. Let the following example suffice: "I know that without me God can live not one instant. Shall I be annihilated, He must give up the Ghost out of need. . . . I am great as God, He is as I so small: He cannot be above me, I cannot be beneath him" (Silesius 1960, p. 30).

56. Cf., for the origin of this idea, Orban 1980, pp. 171–94. The *civitas terrena* is frequently called "huius saeculi civitas" (the city of this temporal world), or again, "civitas diaboli" (the city of the devil), while the only city of God on earth is the *civitas Dei peregrinans* (the city of God on pilgrimage).

57. Matt. 6:24.

58. Matt. 16:19 and par.

59. Cf. the extraordinarily contemporary phrases of a moral dictionary of the seventeenth century by Benedictine Petrus Berchorius: "*Pax imperata* . . . est pax quam principes et magnates imperant subditis suis; nolunt enim quod rebellent contra eos, sed quod pacifice portent tyrannides, quas imponunt. Ista est *pax violenta*. . . . Isti enim volunt, quod subditi erga eos pacem habeant, tamen ad subditos pacem non servant." (*Commanded peace* . . . is the peace that princes and potentates command their subjects; for they will not that they rebel against them, but that they peacefully bear the tyrannies they impose. This is *violent peace.* . . . For they wish that the subjects have peace with respect to them; however, they do not preserve peace toward their subjects.) (Quoted in Janssen 1979, p. 561.)

60. Augustine, *De Civitate Dei,* book 19, chaps. 12, 13.

61. Nicholas of Cusa, *De Concordantia Catholica*, I, 3, 7 (quoted in Janssen 1979, p. 552). (I have been unable to confirm this reference in my edition.)

62. The Council of Chalcedon defined that Christ, the prototype of all reality, was one with the Divinity, "without confusion or mutation, indivisibly and inseparably" (cf. Denzinger, no. 302). The four negative adverbials were very influential in the christian tradition until, perhaps out of a fear of the apophatic, they have become obscured in recent centuries: *asygchytōs (inconfuse), atreptōs (immutabiliter), adiairetōs (indivise),* and *achōristōs (inseparabiliter).*

63. Cf. Panikkar 1963/VI, esp. chap. 5, "La superación del humanismo" ("Transcending Humanism"), pp. 178–253.

64. Benz writes, correctly: "Revolution is the transition from 'awaiting' the Reign of God to an active speeding of its upbuilding through the application of force" (Benz 1978, p. 26).

65. Matt. 4:4 and par.

66. Cf., e.g., John 1:12; Gal. 3:26; Eph. 1:5; etc.

67. Cf. Panikkar 1977/XXV, parts 3 (23, 26), 5 (11), etc.

68. Cf. the Cusan's marvelous response (which we do not reproduce here because it does not directly pertain to our subject) to the text of the following note.

69. "Concedi potest, quod triplex est mundus: parvus, qui homo; maximus, qui est Deus; magnus, qui universum dicitur. Parvus est similitudo magni, magnus similitudo maximi" (Nicholas of Cusa 1960, *De Ludo Globi,* 1:294 [fol. 157r16]; 1967, 3:260).

70. Cf. contemporary efforts to recover the harmony, e.g., Colinas 1991.

71. The last lines of Antonio Machado quoted in chap. 1 above, whose title is "To the Great Plenum or Integral Consciousness," end:

> Harmony!
> All things singing, plain as day.
> Erase all zeros.

Turn again and see,
surging up from its springs,
the living waters of being!

72. Cf. Panikkar 1973/3, which shows the western cultural origin of the concept of "revolution." A certain antecedent philosophy is required even for the word to have meaning.

73. We know of the attitude of certain catholic bishops of North America who, in 1982, refused to pay a portion of their taxes calculated to correspond to arms expenditures, thus disobeying a civil law. Cf. the growing conviction in christian circles that at least nuclear weapons are immoral. Cf. also the second version of the pastoral letter of the North American bishops, dated October 26, 1982, on peace: "We have judged immoral even the threat to use [nuclear] weapons." But they do not want to go to extremes, and the paragraph continues: "At the same time we have held that the possession of nuclear weapons may be tolerated as deterrents while meaningful efforts are underway to achieve multilateral disarmament." The contradiction is immediately evident. Is not "deterrence" precisely a "threat"? "If the threat is immoral, how can the possession not be? Is not the possession the threat?" asks Arthur Jones, writing in the *National Catholic Reporter,* October 29, 1982, p. 20. Cf. further the *Frankfurter Allgemeine Zeitung,* October 23, 1982, p. 12, on the controversy over similar topics in the anglican church.

74. The adage dates from Flavius Vegetius Renatus, *Epitome Rei Militaris,* book 3, Prologue: "Qui desiderat pacem, praeparet bellum."

75. Cf. the European meeting of catholic intellectuals (MICC Pax Romana) in Rome, September 11–14, 1982, with its express opposition to the acceptance of the principle, "Si vis pacem, para bellum."

76. The entire justification of the Gulf War was based on the defense of the status quo of 1990, ignoring the history of the Middle East, not only of the past century, but since World War I.

77. Cf. Panikkar 1961/IV, against nationalism and in favor of love of country in the ancient christian context.

78. Cf., e.g., Everts 1980, Sölle 1983.

PART 3. CULTURAL DISARMAMENT AS PEACE'S REQUIREMENT

1. Cf. "Proceedings of the I Seminario Nazionale di Studi," in Panikkar 1987/C, which gather my presentations, some of which I have used in developing Part 3.

CHAPTER 7. PEACE AS HARMONY, FREEDOM, AND JUSTICE

1. Cf. Panikkar 1981/9.
2. Cf. Lana 1991, p. 158.
3. Cf. Panikkar 1979/XXVII, esp. the first part, pp. 4–184.

4. Terence, *Andria*, I, 1, 34. But Terence has received his motto by way of aphorisms of two of the seven sages of Greece: *Metron ariston*, Cleobulus of Lindus had said—"Measure [moderation, proportion] is best"; and Solon of Athens: "*Méden agan* (Nothing to excess).

5. Goethe, *Faustus*, 350 ("Prolog im Himmel").

6. Dante, *Inferno*, III, 5–6.

7. Cf., obliquely, Ives 1970, who treats Schiller, and Miller 1985, who treats the Vedic harmony.

8. Cf. the chapter, "La armonía invisible," in Panikkar 1990/XXX, pp. 95–152, although the main subject of the chapter is an application to the interreligious encounter.

9. *Vita Pythagorae*, 51, in Porphyry 1987, p. 53.

10. Cf. the expressions, "Trinity" (Father, Son, Spirit), "Triad" (God, world, cosmos), "Trikāla" (past, present, future), "Trimūrti" (Brahmā, Viṣṇu, Śiva), "Triguna" (Sattva, Rajas, Tamas), "Triratna" (Buddha, Dharma, Sangha), "Tribhuvana" (earth, air, sky), "ternary" (subject, verb, object), "Triloka" (the three worlds: heavenly, human, underworld), "Aum," etc., etc.

11. Aurobindo 1955, 1:2.

12. Cf., by way of example, the various contributions in Rouner 1989.

13. Cf. the entry "Libertad" in Ferrater Mora 1984, for a good summary of the general problematic.

14. Cf. Giner 1987.

15. Panikkar 1982/17 and 1990/33.

16. *BG* III, 25: "The wise person ought to act with detachment, concerned only with maintaining the world" (cf. III, 20). Cf. also *MB* XII, 251, 25, where "God" institutes the *dharma* for the *samgraha* of the world. I doubt that Goethe knew this verse of the Gītā when he described the desires of Faust: "That I may know the assembled content of the world's furthermost recesses" (*Faustus*, "Nacht," 382–83).

17. Cf. *MB* VIII, 69.59; XII, 109, 14.

18. Isaiah 32:17 in the Vulgate, which continues: "Et cultus justitiae silentium et securitas usque in sempiternum" (And the worship of justice, calm and safety forever). The biblical text has been variously translated. The very beautiful translation of the Hebrew text by Buber 1985 reads:

> Die Tat der Wahrhaftigkeit wird Friede,
> der Dienst der Wahrhaftigkeit Stillehalt
> und sichere Gelassenheit
> in Weltzeit.

> (The deed of truthfulness is peace,
> and the service of truthfulness, composure
> calm and sure,
> in this life.)

Different overtones!

19. Ps. 85:11, in the Vulgate. (In the New American Bible, "Justice and peace will kiss.")

20. Rom. 14:17.

21. Cf. Pieper 1953, which has become a Thomistic classic valid for many non-Thomists as well.

22. The character of this book does not imply rendering definitive judgment on the examples mentioned, which we are using merely in order to shed light on the complexity of the problems.

23. Cf. Panikkar 1993/XXVIII.

24. Horace's lovely "Paupertas impulit audax ut versus facerem" (Poverty has driven me to be daring enough to write verse)—*Epist.* II, 2, 41—which he wrote when he found that his goods had been confiscated, leaving him in the most absolute need, does not correspond to the reality of true poverty, any more than evangelical poverty (Matt. 5:3) is human misery. Delivered from the superfluous, and reduced to a bare minimum, the daring person can write poetry. But not if he or she is starving to death, is persecuted for a defense of justice, or is shut up in a refugee camp.

25. Cf. Panikkar 1991/16.

26. Cf., still only by way of an example, the article Mosterín 1991, although his recommendation of an army of experts in the science of killing and destruction poses just as many problems, and more serious ones.

27. John of the Cross, always so astonishing when carefully read, in commenting on the first line of the second stanza ("A oscuras y segura") of his *Dark Night of the Soul,* says that to walk in the dark is to walk in safety, "because ordinarily the soul never wanders off course" (II, 16, 2). What causes it to wander are "its appetites or its tastes, or its discourses, or its understandings, or its penchants" (ibid.). And he repeats that, "when the soul walks more *a oscuras,* more in the dark, and empty of its natural operations, it walks more *segura,* more sure" (II, 16, 3). This would be a version of cosmic confidence.

The reader will appreciate our recalling the entire stanza:

> A oscuras y segura,
> por la secreta escala, disfrazada,
> ¡oh dichosa ventura!
> a oscuras y en celada,
> estando ya mi casa sosegada.

> (In darkness and secure,
> by the secret ladder, in disguise—
> oh, happy danger!—
> in darkness and in hiding,
> my house already quiet.)

28. *RV* X, 191, 4. The key word here is *sāmana* (from *sam,* which denotes community, solidarity, conjoint belonging, equality).

For western tradition, cf. Gentili 1973.

Heraclitus: "*Ek tōn diapherontōn kallistēn harmonian*" (Frag. 8), re-
called by Aristotle (*Nichomachaean Ethics*, 2, 1155b4) and Seneca:
"Tota haec mundi concordia ex discordibus constat" (This whole concord of the world consists of discords) (*Naturalium Quaestiones*, VII,
27, 4). Cf. also Heraclitus, Frag. 112.

For *concordia discors*, cf. Bonicatti 1973.

29. The condensed Greek text is almost impossible to translate in a
few words: "*Esti gar harmonia polymige ōn henōsis kai dicha phroneontōn
symphronēsis*" (Frag. 10, in Diels). Capelle 1968 (Frag. 15) very correctly translates: "Harmonie ist Vereinigung des Vielgemischten und
Eintracht des Zwieträchtigen" (Harmony is the unification of the inter-
mingled and the concord of the discordant).

30. Cf. *RV* X, 129, 4; *AV* XIX, 52.

31. Cf. *AV* IX, 2, 19.

32. John Scotus Eriugena, *De Divisione Naturae*, I, 74 (*PL* 122:
519).

33. Aristotle, *Metaphysics*, XII, 7 (1072a26).

34. Dante, *Paradiso*, XXXII, 145.

CHAPTER 8. OBSTACLES TO PEACE

1. We know Gandhi's statement: "The world offers enough to satisfy our needs, but not our greed."

2. Frag. 119.

3. Cf. Dumézil 1958.

4. The *Encyclopaedia Britannica* (1974) has only one article under
"military": "Military Law." The *Encyclopaedia Universalis* (1985) has
two articles, which speak practically only of war. The *International Encyclopaedia of the Social Sciences* (1968) devotes a number of articles to
the subject, but practically all of them bear on modern military organization, and none of them on our first viewpoint. In fact, it is explicitly
stated that "the term 'military' implies an acceptance of organized violence as a legitimate means for realizing social objectives" (Kurt Lang).
On the other hand, the article "Militarismus" in *Geschichtliche Grundbegriffe* (1979) is very interesting. It cites Montesquieu, who in 1748
wrote in his *De l'esprit des Lois*, XIII, 17: "Une maladie nouvelle s'est
répandue en Europe; elle a saisi nos princes et leur fait entretenir un
nombre désordonné de troupes" (vol. 4, p. 8).

5. Virgil, *Aeneid*, book 6, line 832: "Do not instill your minds with
all these wars!"

6. "Artem autem illam mortiferam et Deo odibilem ballistariorum et
sagittariorum, adversus Christianos et Catholicos exerci de cetero sub
anathemate prohibemus" (Alberigo 1973, p. 203). (But the practice of
that deadly art, hateful to God, of missiles and arrows, against christians
and catholics, we forbid under pain of anathema.)

7. As we know, casuistry crept into the interpretation of the Council's

text, and "christian" princes did not regard themselves forbidden to use such arms against infidels and heretics.

8. Cf. a brief summary of aggression from the viewpoint of the history of religions in Gekle 1988.

9. Fromm 1973, p. 215.

10. "The moment one state augments what it calls its troops, the others at once augment theirs." See Montesquieu, quoted in n. 4 above.

11. We need only cite the works of Alexandre Koyré (among them, Koyré 1957) and Werner Marx 1983 in order to span the cosmological and ethical poles of what I mean to indicate: the continuity, desacralizing though it may be, of western civilization.

12. Cf. an amplification of these theses in Panikkar 1984/26; 1991/XXXII, pp. 111–27: "El tecnocentrisme."

13. *Money:* According to data of the International Bank of Regulations for 1992, the amount exchanged in *daily* monetary transactions surpasses $1 trillion—that is, forty to fifty times more than in all daily commercial operations. This quantity is equivalent to one-half the *annual* wealth produced by a rich country like France. Cf. D. Gervais, in *Le Monde Diplomatique,* January 1993, p. 18.

Arms: The defense budget of the United States rose to $291 billion in 1992. But even the SAARC countries (Bangladesh, India, Nepal, Pakistan, Sri Lanka, and Bhutan) spent more than $11.09 billion on weapons in 1986, with an annual increase (from 1973 to 1983) of 5.3 percent, which is a higher rate than in the First World. Cf. *The Times of India,* November 19, 1990. The situation is a global one.

Advertising: North American tobacco companies spend $3.3 billion a year on advertising (*The Boston Globe,* October 4, 1990). The Japanese spend more on advertising than all of China on education or all of the Indian subcontinent (India, Bangladesh, and Sri Lanka) in foreign trade. Cf. *Asiaweek,* June 16, 1989, for many other data.

Tourist industry: Cf., e.g., for revealing data, fascicles 1 and 2 of the *Cultural Survival Quarterly,* 16 (1990): "Breaking Out of the Tourist Trap."

14. For the figures on the world's industrial and consumer capacity, cf. *Le Monde Diplomatique,* December 1992, p. 32.

The U.S. foreign debt has quadrupled in three years. In 1992 it surpassed $4 billion. That same year, the debt of the Third World rose 73 percent. Cf. Claude Julien, writing in *Le Monde Diplomatique,* December 1992, p. 8. Since the foreign debt crisis exploded in 1982, Latin America sent $4 billion monthly (average over 108 months) to the wealthy North. Africa pays some $1 billion a month: Susan George, *Le Monde Diplomatique,* June 1992, supp., p. ii. Cf. other data of the same author in *L'Altra Pagina,* September 1992, p. 7. For more details, cf. *Papeles para la Paz,* esp. no. 24 (1987), R. L. Siward, "Gastos militares y sociales en el mundo"; nos. 31–32 (1988), W. Arkin, "La carrera de armamentos nucleares en el mar"; etc. Cf. also articles in *Bulletin of*

Peace Proposals and in *Journal of Peace Research,* as well as certain issues of the *UNESCO Courier,* e.g., April 1979 (*The Arms Race*); September 1980 (*Disarmament Education: A Farewell to Arms*); March 1982 (*Swords into Plowshares*). The absence of treatments of the subject in more recent years may speak for itself.

Poverty: In Europe, which is not a poor continent, the number of poor has grown since 1975 by some 40 percent. In 1992, wealthy Europe counted 53 million citizens (out of a total of 340 million) who lived below the poverty line (cf. *Le Monde Diplomatique,* July 1992, p. 14). In Africa and Latin America, according to the International Labor Organization, 67 percent of the population are poor, and 39 percent destitute. Cf., e.g., Surin 1989, p. 666, for numerous sources. In the United States, there were 36,600,000 poor in 1990 (cf. *Financial Times,* September 27, 1991, p. 4, which cites official sources). The "poverty line" for this last statistic is based on the standard of a four-person family whose monthly per capita income is $278.

15. After years of using the expression "modern science," I discover that Koyré 1973, p. 289, uses it in this same sense (roughly, science from Galileo to Einstein), and distinguishes it from contemporary and classical (which would be principally that of the Greeks) science. Galileo's intuition was correct: it was a matter of a *new science,* so new that it was no longer *science* in the traditional sense.

16. The author has been preparing for years a book, *The Conflict of Cosmologies.* Cf. Panikkar 1990/22; 1990/24.

17. Cf. Haas 1971.

18. Cf. Panikkar 1977/XXV, pp. 747ff.

19. John 17:3.

20. Cf. Panikkar 1986/13.

21. Aristotle, *Politics,* I, 2 (1253a9).

22. An entire world congress of philosophy was dedicated to this problem. There were readily admitted to be many forms of rationality, but few presentations dared to dethrone reason, without thereby enthroning unreason. Rather than consulting the Acts of the Congress, cf. the 714-page summary of the presentations, *Weltkongress für Philosophie* 1978.

23. Bellet 1979.

24. The bibliography of the theology of liberation is now quite abundant, if still unknown to many thinkers and the world at large. Liberation theology itself has undergone a process of maturation and deepening. Arising out of a christian conscience confronted by institutionalized injustice justified or glossed over by the institutional churches (Gutiérrez 1973, 1982; Pixley and Boff 1986), it has attempted to develop a whole mythology (Sobrino 1982, L. Boff 1983, González Faus 1984), and a philosophy (Dussel 1977), and is now entering the phase of the discovery of its own importance, as in the collective works of Gibellini 1979, Fornet-Betancourt 1991, and Ellacuría-Sobrino 1991.

25. Cf. Luke 18:8.

CHAPTER 9. PATHWAYS TO PEACE

1. Data as found in Clay 1987.

2. "Dem Sieg Geweiht, vom Krieg Zerstört, zum Frieden Mahnend," we read on the new frontispiece of the triumphal arch (*Siegestor*) rebuilt on Munich's Ludwigstrasse after World War II: "Consecrated to Victory, Destroyed by War, Cautioning Peace."

3. Cf. the voluminous and well-documented Fisch 1979.

4. Pope Benedict XV was called "Maledict XV" for having dared, on August 1, 1917, before the end of World War I, to send a letter to all the belligerents urging them to accept a "just and lasting peace," and to abandon the "useless struggle" instead of striving to achieve "victory." John XXIII's encyclical *Pacem in Terris* (April 11, 1963) recalls this letter in a note.

5. Cf., by way of example, the volumes of Amnesty International 1988.

6. Very slowly, by the way. The two phrases sculpted at the beginning of World War II on the statue of Marshal Joffre in front of the Ecole Militaire of Paris, facing the Eiffel Tower, a place visited by thousands of tourists, are such warmongering statements that it is difficult to read them with composure.

7. *Weekly Mail,* January 3, 1992.

8. Cf. Lana 1991, pp. 155ff.

9. On December 24, 1939, when World War II had just begun, Pope Pius XII said, in his Christmas message: "A fundamental postulate of a just and honorable peace is the safeguarding of the right to life and independence of all nations, great and small, powerful and weak." This was the first of the Pontiff's "fundamental points for a just peace." The second is also worthwhile quoting: For "a true peace, nations must be delivered from the heavy servitude of the arms race." And the Pope added: "Peace treaties that would not attribute a fundamental importance to a negotiated, organic, and progressive bilateral disarmament, in the practical order as well as the spiritual, . . . would sooner or later reveal, especially, their inconsistency and want of vitality." (Pius XII 1946, p. 464.) I take the liberty of noting that the pontifical message spoke of *spiritual disarmament.*

10. Cf. Girard 1972, 1985, along with many reactions to his first work. "There is no cheating violence, except by closing off every outlet and giving it something to chew on" (1972, p. 17). His theory could be summed up in his asseveration: "Sacrifice is violence without risk of vengeance" (1972, p. 29).

11. It is worthwhile observing, as a theological explanation in contrast with the Anselmian theory, that Hugo of Saint Victor, in the twelfth century, was able to speak not of a "redemption," but of a

126

"restoration." With a view to recalling this fundamental aspect of christian tradition, and rehabilitating the mystical scholasticism of the Victorines, I take the liberty of quoting this theologian: "Duo enim sunt opera in quibus universa continentur quae facta sunt. Primum est opus conditionis. Secundum est opus restaurationis. . . . Opus conditionis est quo factum est, ut essent quae non erant. . . . Opus restaurationis est quo factum est, ut melius essent quae perierant." (For there are two works in which all things that have been made are contained. The first is the work of founding. The second is the work of restoration. . . . The work of founding is that by which it has come about that things are that were not. . . . The work of restoration is that by which it has come about that things that had perished are better [than before].) (*De Sacramentis Christianae Fidei*, I, prologue, IX, 2 [*PL* 176:183AB].) He calls creation *conditio*, or foundation (cf. the calendric indication, "Ante/Post Urbem [Rome] Conditam"); and he calls redemption *restauratio*, or renewal. He also calls creation *gratia creatrix*, the creative grace (ibid., I, 6, 17 [*PL* 176:273C]).

12. John 20:21–23.

13. It is instructive, and somewhat alarming, to see how little the profound meaning of forgiveness and reconciliation has been studied. Dictionaries of philosophy, for example, leave it practically out of account, and those of theology reduce it to an exegesis on the Sacrament of Penance.

14. Cf. MacIntyre 1982, 1988 for further clarification.

15. Referring to the political order, Jacques 1992 (p. 32) writes: "Forgiveness excuses nothing. It delivers the victim of an obsession from his or her torment and resentment, while the guilty party is called upon to be transformed after having repented."

16. Cf. Panikkar 1984/19.

Bibliography

Acts of the Congress
  1952 Actas del Congreso Eucarístico Internacional, *La Eucaristía y la paz*. Barcelona.
Alberigo, J. [et al.]
  1973 *Conciliorum oecumenicorum decreta*. 3d ed. Bologna: Istituto per le Scienze Religiose.
Amnesty International
  1988 *Informe*. Madrid: EDAI.
Arkin, W.
  1988 "La carrera de armamentos nucleares en el mar," *Papeles para la Paz* 31–32, pp. 3–32.
Atīśa
  1983 *A Lamp for the Path and Commentary (Bodhi-patha-pradīpa)*. Trans. and annotated by R. Sherburne. London: Allen & Unwin.
Augustine
  1946ff. *Obras Completas*. (Works.) Madrid (BAC).
Aurobindo, S.
  1955 *The Life Divine*. Pondicherry: Aurobindo Ashram Press.
Azad, M. A. K. [et al.]
  1952 *History of Philosophy, Eastern and Western*. 2 vols. London: Allen & Unwin.

Barnet, R. J., and R.E. Müller.
  1974 *Global Reach: The Power of the Multinational Corporations*. New York: Simon & Schuster.

Battistelli, F.
1985   *Armi e armamenti: Dagli esplosivi alle testate nucleari. Una possibile strategia di pace.* Rome: Editori Riuniti.
Battistelli, F, G. Mattioli, G. Piana, and A. N. Terrin (eds.)
1988   *Ecologia e Pace.* Il Seminario nazionale di studi Città di Castello. L'altrapagina.
Bellet, M.
1979   *Le Dieu Pervers.* Paris: Desclée.
Benveniste, E.
1969   *Le vocabulaire des institutions indo-européennes.* Paris: Minuit.
Benz, E.
1978   "Zeit, Endheit, Ewigkeit," *Eranos,* 47.
Berger, P. L., and Th. Luckmann.
1966   *The Social Construction of Reality.* Garden City, N.Y.: Doubleday. (*La construcción social de la realidad.* Buenos Aires: Amorrortu, 1968.)
Berten, I., and R. Luneau (eds.)
1991   *Les rendez-vous de Saint-Domingue: Les enjeux d' un anniversaire (1492–1992).* Paris: Centurion.
Birou, A., and P. M. Henry.
1976   *Pour un autre développement.* Paris: Presses Universitaires de France.
Bodin, J.
1958   *Recueils de la Société Jean Bodin.* Brussels: Librarie Encyclopédique.
Boff, L.
1982   *Francisco de Asís: ternura y vigor.* Santander: Sal Terrae. (Trans. *São Francisco de Assis: ternura e vigor,* Petrópolis: Vozes, 1981.)
1983   *Jesucristo el Liberador: Ensayo de cristología crítica para nuestro tiempo.* Santander: Sal Terrae.
Bonicatti, M.
1973   "Chronos—Tyché—Melancholia." In Castelli 1973, pp. 119–34.
Brunner, O. [et al.]
1979   *Geschichtliche Grundbegriffe.* Stuttgart: Klett-Cotta.
Buber, M., and F. Rosenzweig.
1987 (1954)   *Die Schrift.* 11th ed. 4 vols. Heidelberg: Schneider.
Bulletin of Peace Proposals
   Oslo.

Cancik, H. [et al.]
1988   *Handbuch religionswissenschaftlicher Grundbegriffe.* Stuttgart: Kohlhammer.
Capelle, W.
1968   *Die Vorsokratiker.* Stuttgart: Kröner.

Castelli, E. (ed.)
   1973   *Il simbolismo del tempo*. Rome: Istituto di Studi Filosofici.
Chantraine, P.
   1968   *Dictionnaire étymologique de la langue grecque*. Paris: Klinck-
          sieck.
Clay, J.
   1987   "Armed Struggle and Indigenous People," *Cultural Survival
          Quarterly* XI/4, pp. 2–4.
Colinas, A.
   1991   *Tratado de armonía*. Barcelona: Tusquets.
Cortesi, L. (ed.)
   1985   *Guerra e Pace nel mondo contemporaneo*. Naples: Istituto
          Universitario Orientale.
Cortina, A.
   1991   *La moral del camaleón*. Madrid: Espasa-Calpe.

Dictionnaire de Spiritualité
   1983   Paris: Beauchesne.
Diels, H., and W. Kranz.
   1960   *Die Fragmente der Vorsokratiker*. Berlin: Weidmann (1952;
          and later editions).
Díez Alegría, J. M.
   1968   "Gerechtigkeit," *Sacramentum Mundi*. Freiburg: Herder.
Dizionario Enciclopedico di Spiritualità
   1975   Rome: Studium.
Drewermann, E.
   1992   *Die Spirale der Angst: Der Krieg und das Christentum*. Frei-
          burg: Herder.
Dumézil, G.
   1958   *L'idéologie tripartie des indo-européens*. Brussels (Col. Ato-
          mus, vol. 31).
Dussel, E.
   1977   *Filosofía de la liberación*. Mexico: Edicol.
   1985   *Philosophy of Liberation*. Maryknoll, N.Y.: Orbis.

Eliade, M.
   1949   *Le mythe de l'éternel retour: archétypes et répétition*. Paris: Gal-
          limard.
Ellacuría, I., and J. Sobrino.
   1991   *Mysterim Liberationis*. Madrid: Trotta.
Enciclopedia Filosofica
   1979   2d ed. Centro di Studi Filosofici di Gallarate.
Encyclopaedia Universalis
   1985   Paris.
Eranos
   1978   *Zeit und Zeitlosigkeit*. Frankfurt: Insel.

Erler, B.
  1987 *L'aide qui tue*. Paris: d'En Bas.
Everts, P. P.
  1980 "Reviving Unilateralism," *Bulletin of Peace Proposals* XI/1,
         pp. 40–56.
Éxodo
  Madrid.

Falk, R., S. S. Kim, and S. H. Mendlovitz (eds.)
  1982 *Toward a Just World Order*. Vol. I. Boulder, Colo: Westview
         Press.
Ferrater Mora, J.
  1984 *Diccionario de Filosofía*. 5th ed. Madrid: Alianza.
Fisch, J.
  1979 *Krieg und Frieden im Friedensvertrag*. Stuttgart: Ernst Klett.
Fornet-Betancourt, R. (ed.)
  1991 *Verändert der Glaube die Wirtschaft? Theologie und Ökonomie
         in Lateinamerika*. Freiburg: Herder.
Foulquié, P.
  1962 *Dictionnaire de la langue philosophique*. Paris: PUF.
Fromm, E.
  1973 *The Anatomy of Human Destructiveness*. New York: Holt,
         Rinehart & Winston.

Gabriel, L. See Nicholas of Cusa.
Galtung, J.
  1987 *United States Foreign Policy: As Manifest Theology*. IGCC Pol-
         icy Paper, no. 4. University of California.
Gekle, H.
  1988 "Militarismus." In Cancik 1988, vol. I, pp. 394–406.
Gentili, A.
  1973 "Problemi del simbolismo armonico nella cultura elisabet-
         tiana." In Castelli (ed.) 1973, pp. 59–102.
George, S.
  1976 *How the Other Half Dies: The Real Reasons for World Hunger*.
         New York: Penguin Books.
Geschichtliche Grundbegriffe. See Brunner 1979.
Gibellini, B. (ed.)
  1979 *Frontiers of Theology in Latin America*. Maryknoll, N.Y.: Or-
         bis. (*Le nuove frontiere della teologia in America Latina*. Bres-
         cia: Queriniana, 1975.)
Giner, S.
  1987 *El destino de la libertad*. Madrid: Espasa-Calpe.
Girard, R.
  1972 *La violence et le sacré*. Paris: Bernard Grasset.
  1985 *La route antique des hommes pervers*. Paris: Grasset.

Gonzàlez Faus, J. I.
1984   *La humanidad nueva: Ensayo de Cristología*. Santander: Sal Terrae.

Grumbrecht, H. W.
1979   "Modern, Modernität, Moderne." In Brunner 1979, vol. 4.

Guardini, R.
1950   *Das Ende der Neuzeit*. Würzburg.

Guthrie, K. S.
1987   *Pythagorean Sourcebook and Library*. Comp. and trans. Grand Rapids: Phanes.

Gutiérrez, G.
1973   *Teología de la liberación*. Salamanca: Sígueme. (ET: *A Theology of Liberation*. Maryknoll, N.Y.: Orbis, 1973.)
1982   *La fuerza històrica de los pobres*. Salamanca: Sígueme.

Haas, A. M.
1971   *Nim din selbes war*. Fribourg: Universitäts-Verlag.

Hart, J.
1984   *The Spirit of the Earth*. New York: Paulist.

Hassler, H.-J., and H. Kauffmann (eds.)
1986   *Kultur gegen Krieg*. Cologne: Pahl-Rugenstein.

Hastings, J.
1917   *Encyclopedia of Religion and Ethics*. Edinburgh: T.&T. Clark.

Hawking, S. W.
1988   *A Brief History of Time*. Toronto: Bantam. (*Historia del tiempo*. Barcelona: Crítica, 1989.)

Heer, F.
1953   *Europäische Geistesgeschichte*. Stuttgart: Kohlhammer.
1980   *Europa, madre de revoluciones*. 2 vols. Madrid: Alianza.

Heidegger, M.
1967   *Vorträge und Aufsätze*. Pfullingen: Neske.

Heilbronner, R. L.
1974   *An Inquiry into the Human Prospect*. New York: Norton.

Heim, F.
1992   *La théologie de la victoire*. Paris: Beauchesne.

Holl, K.
1978   "Pazifismus." In *Geschichtliche Grundbegriffe*, vol. 4, pp. 767–87.

Hornung, E.
1978   "Zeitliches Jenseits im Alten Ägypten," *Eranos* 47.

Huber, W.
"Friedensforschung." In Ritter 1972.

Institute for World Order (ed.)
1981   *Peace and World Order Studies*. New York: Transnational Academic Program.

Ives, M. C.
   1970   *The Analogy of Harmony*. Pittsburgh: Duquesne University Press.

Jacques, A.
   1992   "Impunité et fausses paix," *Le Monde Diplomatique* (Sept.),
          p. 32.
Janssen, W.
   1979   "Friede." Cf. Brunner 1979, pp. 543–91.
Jaspers, K.
   1960   *Die Atombombe und die Zukunft des Menschen* (1958). Mu-
          nich: Pieper.
Journal of Peace Research
   Oslo.
Juan de la Cruz
   1975   *Vida y obras de San Juan de la Cruz*. 9th ed. Madrid: BAC.

Kant, I.
   1795   *Zum ewigen Frieden*. Königsberg: F. Nicolovius.
Kennedy, G.
   1975   *The Military in the Third World*. New York: Scribner.
Keynes, J. M.
   1920   *The Economic Consequences of the Peace*. New York: Harcourt,
          Brace.
König, F.
   1956   *Religionswissenschaftliches Wörterbuch*. Freiburg: Herder.
Koyré, A.
   1957   *From the Closed World to the Infinite Universe*. New York:
          Harper.
   1973   *Etudes d'histoire de la pensée scientifique*. Paris: Gallimard.

Ladrière, J.
   1977   *The Challenge Presented to Cultures by Science and Technology*.
          Paris: UNESCO.
Lalande, A.
   1980   *Vocabulaire technique et critique de la Philosophie*. Paris: PUF.
Lana, I.
   1991   *L'idea della pace nell' antichità*. S. Domenico di Fiesole, Flor-
          ence: Edizioni Cultura della Pace.
Landgren-Baekstroem, S.
   1982   "Global Arms Trade," *Bulletin of Peace Proposals* XIII/3, pp.
          201–10.
Latouche, S.
   1991   *La planète des naufragés*. Paris: La Découverte.
La Valle, R.
   1990   "E Dio dov'era?" *Bozze* 90, pp. 5–38.
   1991   "La pace come riforma istituzionale e politica," *Bozze* 91, pp. 5–
          19.

Lercaro, G.
   1983   "La pace come testimonianza evangelica," *Cristianesimo nella storia,* IV/2 (Oct.), pp. 468–69.
Liedke, G. (ed.)
   1972   *Frieden, Bibel, Kirche.* Studien zur Friedensforschung, vol. 9. Stuttgart: Klett; Munich: Kösel.
López de Romaña, A.
   1989   "The Autonomous Economy," *Inter-culture* 104, 3/4, pp. 2–169.
Lücker, M. A. (ed.)
   1980   *Den Frieden tun (Die 3. Weltversammlung der Religionen für den Frieden).* Freiburg: Herder.
Luti, G.
   1987   *L'utopia della pace nella Resistenza.* S. Domenico di Fiesole, Florence: Edizioni Cultura della Pace.

MacIntyre, A.
   1982   *After Virtue: A Study in Moral Theory.* London: Duckworth.
   1988   *Whose Justice? Which Rationality?* London: Duckworth.
Mannheim, K.
   1964   *Wissenssoziologie.* Neuwied: Luchterhand.
Marx, W.
   1983   *Gibt es auf Erden ein Mass?* Hamburg: Felix Meiner.
Mate, R.
   1990   *Mística y política.* Estella: Verbo Divino.
McGovern, A. F.
   1985   *Theology Digest,* vol. 32, no. 2 (summer), pp. 103–7.
Miller, J.
   1985   *The Vision of Cosmic Order in the Vedas.* London: Routledge & Kegan Paul.
Molinos, M. de
   1976   *Guía espiritual.* Madrid: Universidad Pontificia de Salamanca.
Mosterín, J.
   1991   "El secuestro militar," *El País* (Madrid), July 7, p. 14.

Nebbia, G.
   1991   *Lo sviluppo sostenibile.* S. Domenico di Fiesole, Florence: Edizioni Cultura della Pace.
Nicholas of Cusa
   1960   *Cusanus Konkordanz.* Ed. E. Zellinger. Munich: Hueber.
   1967   *Philosophisch-Teologische Schriften.* Ed. Leo Gabriel. 3 vols. Vienna: Herder.
Nietzsche, F.
   1966   *Zur Genealogie der Moral.* Werke, ed. K. Schlechta. Munich: Hanser. (ET: *The Genealogy of Morals.*)

135

Orban, A. P.
    1980   "Ursprung und Inhalt der Zwei-Staaten-Lehre in Augustinus 'De civitate Dei,'" *Archiv für Begriffsgeschichte* XXIV/2, pp. 171–94.

Panikkar, R.
    1961/IV   *Patriotismo y cristianidad.* Madrid: Rialp.
    1961/15   "La demitologizzazione nell'incontro tra cristianesimo e induismo." In *Il problema della demitizzazione.* Ed. E. Castelli. Padua: CEDAM. Pp. 243–66.
    1963/V   *Ontonomía de la ciencia.* Madrid: Gredos.
    1963/VI   *Humanismo y Cruz.* Madrid: Rialp.
    1965/IX   *Religión y religiones.* Madrid: Gredos.
    1967/XV   *Técnica y tiempo.* Buenos Aires: Columba.
    1971/XII   *Misterio y revelación.* Madrid: Marova.
    1973/3   "Philosophy and Revolution," *Philosophy East and West* (Honolulu) XXIII/3, pp. 315–22.
    1975/1   "El presente tempiterno." In *Teología y mundo contemporáneo.* Ed. A. Vargas-Machuca. Madrid: Cristiandad. Pp. 133–75.
    1977/16   "Colligite Fragmenta: For an Integration of Reality." In *From Alienation to At-One-ness.* Ed. F. A. Eigo and S. E. Fittipaldi. Villanova, Pa.: Villanova University Press. Pp. 19–91.
    1977/XXV   *The Vedic Experience: Mantramañjarī.* Berkeley: University of California Press; London: Darton, Longman & Todd.
    1978/1   "Religion ou Politique?" *Archivo di Filosofia.* Ed. M. M. Olivetti. Rome: Istituto di Studi Filosofici. Pp. 73–82. (Also in *Religion and Society* XXV/3 (September 1978); *Encuentro islamo-cristiano* (Madrid) 1991, no. 230, pp. 1–10.
    1978/2   "Non Dualistic Relation between Religion and Politics" *Religion and Society* XXV/3 (September 1978).
    1979/XXII   *Culto y secularización.* Madrid: Marova.
    1979/XXVII   *Myth, Faith and Hermeneutics.* New York: Paulist.
    1981/9   "Per una lettura trasculturale del simbolo." *Quaderni di psicoterapia infantile.* Rome: Borla. Pp. 53–91.
    1981/10   "Is History the Measure of Man?" *Teilhard Review* (London) XVI/1, 2, pp. 39–45.
    1982/17   "Alternative(s) à la culture moderne," *Interculture* (Montreal) 77, pp. 5–25.
    1982/18   "Cross-cultural Economics," *Interculture* (Montreal) 77, pp. 26–68.
    1983/11   "The End of History: The Threefold Structure of Human Time-Consciousness." In *Teilhard and the Unity of Knowledge.* Ed. T. M. King and J. F. Salmon. New York: Paulist. Pp. 83–141.

1984/3 "L'intuïció cosmoteàndrica," *Qüestions de Vida Cristiana* (Montserrat) 120, pp. 85–91.

1984/19 "The Dialogical Dialogue." In *The World's Religious Traditions.* Ed. F. Whaling. Edinburgh: T. & T. Clark. Pp. 201–21.

1984/20 "La pau politica com objectiu religiós," *Qüestions de Vida Cristiana* (Montserrat) 121, pp. 86–95.

1984/26 "L'émancipation de la technologie," *Interculture* (Montreal) 85, pp. 22–37.

1986/13 "La dialéctica de la razón armada," *Concordia* (Frankfurt) 9, pp. 68–89.

1986/14 "Medicina y Religión," *Jano* (Madrid) XXI/737, pp. 12–48.

1987/C (ed.) *Pace e disarmo culturale.* I seminario nazionale di studi Città di Castello, 28–29, June 1986, Città di Castello (Amministrazione Comunale, L'altrapagina).

1988/20 "La religión del futuro," *Biblia y Fe* (Madrid) XIV/40, pp. 117–41.

1989/17 "Mythos und Logos." In *Geist und Natur.* Ed. H. P. Dürr and W. Ch. Zimmerli. Bern, Munich, Vienna: Scherz. Pp. 206–20.

1990/XXX *Sobre el diálogo intercultural.* Salamanca: San Esteban.

1990/22 "Antinomias entre las cosmologías modernas y las cosmologías tradicionales," *Papeles de la India* (Delhi) XIX/3, pp. 5–13.

1990/24 "Cosmic Evolution, Human History and Trinitarian Life," *The Teilhard Review* (London) XXV/3, pp. 62–71.

1990/33 "Thinking and Being." In *Du Vrai, Du Beau, Du Bien.* Paris: Vrin. Pp. 39–42.

1991/14 "La visió cosmoteàndrica: el sentit religiós emergent del tercer milleni," *Qüestions de Vida Cristiana* (Montserrat) 156, pp. 78–102.

1991/16 "La legitimidad no es la justicia," *El Ciervo* (Barcelona) XL/482, pp. 15–16.

1991/48 "Ecosofia." In *Qüestions de Vida Cristiana* (Montserrat) 158, pp. 66–79.

1991/XXXII *La nova innocencia.* Barcelona: Llar del Llibre.

1993/XXVIII *Blessed Simplicity: The Monk as Universal Archetype.* New York: Seabury.

1993/XXXIII *The Cosmotheandric Experience.* Maryknoll, N.Y.: Orbis.

1993/XXXIV *Ecosofia: la nuova sagezza.* Assisi: Citadella.

1995/LX *Il "daîmon" della politica.* Bologna: EDB.

Panunzio, S.

1982 "Qual è la guerra giusta?" *Metapolitica* (Rome) VII/2, June 29.

Papeles para la Paz

Madrid: Centro de Investigación para la Paz.

Peace through Religion
  1977   *A Brief Report of the Asian Conference on Religions and Peace*
         (Singapore 1976). Tokyo: Asian Conference on Religion and
         Peace.
Peña, J. de la
  1982   *Corpus Hispanorum de pace,* vol. IX, Madrid: CSIC. See the
         remaining volumes edited by L. Pereña.
Perroux, F.
  1983   *A New Concept of Development: Basic Tenets.* London: Croom
         Helm; Paris: UNESCO.
Pestalozzi, H. A. [et al.]
  1982   *Frieden in Deutschland.* Munich: W. Goldmann.
Philberth, B.
  1963   *Christliche Prophetie und Nuklearenergie.* Zurich: Christiana.
Pieper, J.
  1953   *Über die Gerechtigkeit.* Munich: Kösel.
Pius XII
  1946   *Discursos y mensajes de su Santidad.* Vol. I. Madrid: Acción
         Católica Española.
Pixley, J., and C. Boff
  1986   *Opção pelos pobres.* Petrópolis: Vozes.
Polany, K.
  1957   *The Great Transformation.* Boston: Beacon.
Porphyry
  1987   *Vita Pythagorae.* Trans. M. Periago Lorente. Madrid: Gredos.
Pross, H.
  1983   *La violencia de los símbolos sociales.* Barcelona: Anthropos.
Puig i Boix, J.
  1991   *L'Ecologisme.* Barcelona: Barcanova.

Rahnema, M.
  1991   "Global Poverty: A Pauperizing Myth," *Interculture*
         XXIV/2, no. 3 (spring).
Reding, J.
  1986   *Friedensstifter—Friedensboten.* Recklinghausen: Georg Bitter.
Regamey, P.
  1958   *Non-violence et conscience chrétienne.* Paris: Cerf.
Religion in Geschichte und Gegenwart, Die
  1958   Tübingen: Mohr.
Ricca, P.
  1989   *Le chiese evangeliche e la pace.* S. Domenico di Fiesole, Flor-
         ence: Edizioni Cultura della Pace.
Ritter, J. (ed.)
  1972   *Historisches Wörterbuch der Philosophie.* Darmstadt: Wissen-
         schaftliche Buchgesellschaft.

Rosenthal, M., and P. Yudin (eds.)
1967 *A Dictionary of Philosophy.* Moscow: Progress.
Rouner, L. S.
1989 *On Freedom.* Notre Dame, Ind.: University of Notre Dame Press.

Sachs, W.
1992 *The Development Dictionary: A Guide to Knowledge as Power.* London: Zed Books.
Sacramentum Mundi
1968 (Encyclopedia of theology.) Freiburg: Herder.
Scheler, M.
1924 *Versuche zu einer Soziologie des Wissens.* Munich and Leipzig: Duncker & Humblot.
Schell, J.
1982 *The Fate of the Earth.* New York: Knopf. (*El destino de la tierra.* Barcelona: Argos Vergara.)
Schlechta, K.
1966 See Nietzsche 1966.
Schmid, H. H.
1971a *Frieden ohne Illusionen. Die Bedeutung des Begriffs 'schalom' als Grundlage für eine Theologie des Friedens.* Zurich: Theologischer Verlag.
1971b *Schalom. Frieden im Alten Orient und Alten Testament. Stuttgarter Bibel-Studien,* 51. Stuttgart: Katholisches Bibelwerk.
1974 *Altorientalische Welt in der alttestamentlichen Theologie.* Zurich: Theologischer Verlag.
Schwally, F.
1901 *Semitische Kriegsaltertümer.* Leipzig (n.p.).
Sherburne, R. See Atīśa.
Siguán, M. (ed.)
1989 *Philosophia pacis. Homenaje a Raimon Panikkar.* Madrid: Símbolo.
Silesius, A.
1960 *Der cherubinische Wandersmann.* Ed. Ch. Waldemar. Munich: Goldmann.
Sils, D. L. (ed.)
1968 *International Encyclopedia of the Social Sciences.* London: Macmillan & Co. and Free Press.
Siward, R. L.
1983 *World Military and Social Expenditures.* Washington, D.C.: World Priorities.
1987 "Gastos militares y sociales en el mundo," *Papeles para la Paz* 24, pp. 3–16.
Sobrino, J.
1982 *Jesús en America Latina.* Santander: Sal Terrae.

Sölle, D.
  1983   "Unilaterally for Peace," *Cross Currents* (West Nyack, N.Y.)
         XXXIII/2, pp. 140–46.
Surin, K.
  1989   "Towards a 'materialist' critique of 'religious pluralism': a
         polemical examination of the discourse of John Hick and Wil-
         fred Cantwell Smith," *The Thomist* 53/4, pp. 655–73.
Swain, J. C.
  1982   *War, Peace and the Bible.* New York: Orbis Books.

Thomas Aquinas
  1962   *Summa Theologiae.* Rome: Paoline.
Tribunal contra la Guerra del Golfo
  1992   *La Guerra del Golfo un año después.* Madrid: Nueva Utopía.

UNESCO
  The UNESCO Courier. In 24 languages. Paris.
  1981   *Cultural Development—Some Regional Experiences.* Paris:
         UNESCO Press.
  1984a *Stratégies du développement endogène.* Symposium. Paris:
         UNESCO.
  1984b *Historia y diversidad de las culturas.* Symposium. Paris:
         UNESCO; Barcelona: Serbal.

Vachon, R.
  1988   *Alternatives au développement.* Montreal: Centre Intercul-
         turel Monchanin.
Varios
  1952   *La Eucaristía y la paz.* Barcelona: Congreso Eucarístico In-
         ternacional.
Verhelst, T. G.
  1990   *No Life without Roots.* London and New York: Zed Books.
Vittachi, A.
  1989   *Earth Conference One—Sharing a Vision for One Planet.*
         Boston: Shambala.

Weizsäcker, C. F. von
  1948   *Die Geschichte der Natur.* Göttingen: Vandenhoeck &
         Ruprecht.
Weltkongress für Philosophie
  1978   A. Diemer, ed. *Sektion—Vorträge.* Düsseldorf.

Index of Authors

Aristotle, 24, 81, 88, 123 nn.28, 33; 125 n.21
Ashoka, 23
Atīśa, 39, 113 n.18
Augustine of Hippo, 5, 41, 61, 63, 72, 91, 96, 113 n.30, 117 n.38, 119 n.60
Aurobindo, Sri, 66

Benedict XV, pope, 126 n.4
Benz, E. 116 n.24, 119 n.64
Berchorius, P., 119 n.59
Bisser, E., 110 n.1
Bodin, J., 46
Bonaventure, 24
Buber, M., 121 n.18
Bultmann, R., 110 n.38

Catherine of Genoa, 65
Charles V, 97, 106 n.4
Cicero, 13, 14, 39
Cortina, A., 112 n.11

Dante, 65, 76, 121 n.6, 123 n.34
Descartes, R., 8, 96
Dumézil, G., 80

Erasmus, 22, 23

Fichte, J. G., 46
Francis of Assisi, 39
Francisco de Vitoria, 106 n.4
Fromm, E., 82

Galileo, 125 n.15
Galtung, J., 110 n.2, 114 n.33
Gandhi, M. K., 123 n.1
Girard, R., 126 n.10
Goethe, J. W. von, 121 nn.5, 16
Guardini, R., 113 n.22
Gutiérrez, G., 112

Hammurabi, 94, 95
Hegel, G.W.F., 89
Heidegger, M., 113 n.29
Heraclitus, 74, 79, 123 n.28
Hobbes, T., 46, 115 n.12
Homer, 81
Horace, 114 n.1, 122 n.24
Hugo Cardinalis, 108 n.18
Hugo of Saint Victor, 126 n.11

Ignatius of Antioch, 1